ROUTLEDGE LIBRARY EDITIONS:
DEVELOPMENT

DEVELOPMENT AND THE DEBT TRAP

DEVELOPMENT AND THE DEBT TRAP

Economic Planning and External Borrowing in Ghana

ANDRZEJ KRASSOWSKI

Volume 15

Routledge
Taylor & Francis Group
LONDON AND NEW YORK

First published in 1974

This edition first published in 2011
by Routledge
2 Park Square, Milton Park, Abingdon, Oxfordshire OX14 4RN

Simultaneously published in the USA and Canada
by Routledge
711 Third Avenue, New York, NY 10017

First issued in paperback 2014

Routledge is an imprint of the Taylor & Francis Group, an informa business

British Library Cataloguing in Publication Data
A catalogue record for this book is available from the British Library

ISBN13: 978-0-415-58414-2 (Set)
ISBN 13: 978-0-415-59282-6 (hbk)
ISBN 13: 978-0-415-84835-0 (pbk)

Publisher's Note
The publisher has gone to great lengths to ensure the quality of this reprint but points out that some imperfections in the original copies may be apparent.

Disclaimer
The publisher has made every effort to trace copyright holders and welcomes correspondence from those they have been unable to contact.

Development and the Debt Trap

Economic Planning and External Borrowing in Ghana

ANDRZEJ KRASSOWSKI

CROOM HELM LONDON
in association with
THE OVERSEAS DEVELOPMENT INSTITUTE

First published 1974

Croom Helm Ltd
2–10 St. Johns Road, London SW11

ISBN 0–85664–063–8

Printed and bound
in Great Britain by
REDWOOD BURN LIMITED
Trowbridge & Esher.

Contents

Note

All figures are expressed in £ sterling at a constant exchange rate of £1 = £1 (Ghana) = N₵2 = \$2.8. For conversion rates to be used in comparing these figures with figures published elsewhere, particularly those compiled between mid-July 1967 (first Cedi devaluation) and December 1972, see Appendix – Currency and exchange rates.

List of Tables

List of Tables

List of Tables

Table		
2.1	[illegible] public investment [illegible] Ten-Year [illegible]	[illegible]
2.2	Proposed sources of finance for the Ten-Year Plan	[illegible]
3.1	Planned distribution of public investment under the Five-Year Plan	38
3.2	The Volta River Project	[illegible]
4.1	Differences in the sectoral allocations in public investment between the Five-Year and Seven-Year Plans	63
4.2	The importance of public investment in agriculture and industry, and in state enterprises in relation to external capital [illegible], 1958–61 and 1962–5	[illegible]
4.3	Foreign grants, loans and credits extended to Ghana: agreements and gross disbursement, 1950–70	74
5.1	Changes in the sectoral structure of incomes and employment between 1950–[illegible] and 1962–5	99
5.2	Changes in the importance of the public sector between 1950–[illegible] and 1962–5	102
6.1	Western suppliers' credits: new payment schedules 1966 and 1968	130
6.2	Ghana's import structure, [illegible]	136
6.3	New aid commitments and disbursements, 1966–70	138
6.4	Summary outcome of post-Nkrumah external debt negotiations, 1966–70	[illegible]

Appendix

A1	Trends in employment 1950–65	156
A2	Gross Domestic Product, 1950–69	156
A3	Sectoral structure of incomes 1950–[illegible]	157
A4	The public sector in the economy 1950–69	158
A5	Changes in the sectoral distribution of public expenditure 1950–69	159
A6	Sectoral distribution of public investment under the Ten-Year, Five-Year and Seven-Year Plans and in the post-Nkrumah period	160
A7	Composition of government revenue 1950–69	161
A8	Summary of central government budgetary position 1950–69	162
A9	Ghana's foreign trade, 1950–69	163
A10	Summary of the balance of payments and reserve position 1950–69	164

Acknowledgements

In preparing this study I have drawn liberally on facts and comments supplied by officials, of either national governments or international organisations, and many others who were personally involved in the events here described. It is customary in such cases not to single out or identify individuals; so I can only acknowledge my considerable overall debt to them as a group. I am also indebted to very many Ghanaians, holding no particular positions of authority, who helped me to get a glimpse at the grass roots of their country's development. Finally, I acknowledge my special debt to William Clark, first Director of ODI, under whose auspices this study was begun, to Antony Tasker, the present Director, and all my colleagues at ODI, and also to Norman Uphoff, for their support, advice and critical reading of earlier drafts. But no one except myself has any responsibility for my interpretation of the attitudes and policies here described, for errors of fact which the study may still contain, or for its conclusions.

Chapter 1 Introduction

This is an account of how Ghana got into debt and how it has been trying to get out of debt. The account has been compiled with two main purposes. First, it is offered as background to the state of play following Colonel Acheampong's partial repudiation of the debt in January 1972, and the positions taken up by the various protagonists involved in the dispute it provoked. Second, there are lessons to be drawn from Ghana's experience which may be of interest to those concerned with the implications for developing countries of the growing use of medium-term supplier credits, and to those who offer, insure and accept these credits, or have to rescue countries which overburden themselves with debt.

Ghana's debt is the best known of the legacies left from the Nkrumah era. Also, since his downfall the debt has dominated Ghana's internal economic debate – and even its political course – and has stood at the very centre of Ghana's relations with the major Western industrial countries and international financial organisations. Britain, as the former colonial authority and by far the major creditor, and more recently as convenor of the various debt-rescheduling conferences, has had a special responsibility and influence, and its attitude continues to be of importance.

The first two successor regimes to Nkrumah, the National Liberation Council headed successively by Generals Ankrah and Afrifa, and (between August 1969 and January 1972) the elected civilian administration under Dr. Busia, argued the need for generous and long-term debt-relief and aid. Ghana's main creditors have been anxious, however, not to concede anything that might encourage other countries facing mounting debt problems to look for easy remedies through debt-relief or refinancing aid. While the creditors were initially prepared to accept that the debt was an obstacle to Ghana's economic recovery programme, they did not subscribe to the Ghanaian view that it was the main obstacle. As time elapsed after Nkrumah's downfall, creditors became increasingly disappointed by Ghana's performance, which they ascribed largely to internal failings; and their attitude to debt-relief hardened correspondingly.

At dispute throughout the post-Nkrumah period was the real burden of the inherited debt, rather than the immediate financial problem it posed. The facts of the dispute are examined here in some detail, but no attempt is made to provide a project-by-project assessment of the effects of credit-financed schemes on the economy: such an approach is far beyond the capacity of available statistics. In any case, even a successful assessment of this kind could offer only an incomplete view of the debt-burden. The failure of many credit-financed projects was merely the tip of the iceberg, the obvious part of the problem which Nkrumah's policies created. The credit contracts were themselves also only one part of a final phase, although a part which had an important impact on that particular phase, of a fifteen-year period during which Nkrumah fumbled towards an ill-defined goal of economic 'restructuring' based on massive public spending and increasing emphasis on state enterprise in agriculture and industry. The account, therefore, goes back to the roots of these policies and follows them through to the point where external credits became important.

In this way both the credits and the debt which resulted are set in an overall economic and policy context. Moreover, Ghana's experience with other types of external resources – including private investment – and its failure under Nkrumah to establish fruitful relations with Western aid donors, (other than in the context of the Volta Project) influenced the course of economic policy and the eventual reliance on medium-term credits, from both private Western suppliers and East European governments. Some attention is, therefore, also given to putting the medium-term credits in the context of all actual and potential external resources available to Ghana during the entire Nkrumah period.

An attempt has been made to compile statistics on the major strategic aspects of the Ghana economy going back to 1950, the year before Nkrumah first entered government. It is hoped, through this, to illustrate Ghana's development over the entire Nkrumah period (and also that under the NLC) against which Nkrumah's achievements and failings may be more easily judged and the burden of the debt, the NLC's success in coping with it, and the attitude of creditors and donors assessed. But a note of caution must be included here on the statistics which have been assembled. Their coverage and reliability is not always as good as one would wish, particularly before 1955 and after 1965, and they must, therefore, be taken as no more than illustrations of general trends and relative magnitudes.[1]

Notes

1. Attention is drawn to the Statistical Appendix, particularly the notes on Ghana's statistics and exchange rates.

Chapter 2 The Root of the Problem: Economic and Political Conditions and Objectives in the Decade before Independence

1. Strengths and weaknesses of Ghana's economy in the run-up to the 1951 elections

In 1950 Ghana's GDP was just over £22m., its population roughly 5m.; the average GDP per inhabitant was thus in the region of £40, equivalent to very roughly £100 of purchasing power in Britain in 1970. While low by the standards of developed countries, Ghana's income was high among developing countries: it was about the same as that of Malaya, Morocco or Peru, and between two and three times higher than that of India or Indonesia. Among emergent Black African states, only Gabon and French Somalia exceeded Ghana's GDP per head; and even there, if one discounts the higher incomes of the relatively large white communities, the average incomes of Africans were lower than those in Ghana. Among British colonies in Africa, only Zambia (with about £35) came within range of Ghana's income; while that of Uganda was about half, that of the remainder of East Africa between one-half and one-third, and that of Nigeria about one-third.

Ghana's high income offered a considerable savings potential which could be mobilised for financing investment. The development that had taken place had been geographically dispersed, without over-concentration on Accra, the capital, or imbalance in rural-urban incomes – due largely to the remarkable success of the cocoa industry.

Throughout the 1940s Ghana had managed to balance its external and budgetary accounts without too much difficulty, and with a sufficient margin to build up external reserves, which stood at £113m. at the end of 1950. It had got by without British subsidies for its recurrent budget and made only small claims on colonial aid funds (see p.). Its sound financial and external position gave it the appearance of a well-managed economy.

After cocoa, Ghana's biggest asset was the skill of its population. By African standards, the education system was well-developed. In 1950 about one-fifth of children in the relevant age groups attended primary or middle school, a much higher proportion than in other parts of West, East and Southern Africa. Some 3,500 were in secondary schools, more in relation to the population than anywhere else in Black Africa. A

further 2,000 were enrolled in teacher training institutions and 200 in the local university. Of the adult population, some 15,000 had received at least some secondary education, and up to 4,000 had attended teacher training institutions. Some 1,000 Ghanaians had been to university (largely overseas), also the highest number in relation to population anywhere in Black Africa.

In middle-level skills Ghana was reasonably well-off compared to other parts of Africa. While only some 1,000 Ghanaians were following technical or vocational courses, the supply of craftsmen and technicians was adequate for the pace of development in the 1940s. There were, nevertheless, specific shortages, in the building trades for instance, and, most notably, of suitably qualified and experienced men for supervisory grades, such as gang-leaders and foremen. The secondary schools supplied adequate numbers able to cope with general clerical duties, but there was an acute shortage of qualified candidates for posts requiring specific skills, such as book-keeping or even typing.

At the higher skill and professional levels, expatriates were indispensable in both the public and private sectors, particularly in the managerial and technical fields – from tug-pilots and harbour masters to agriculturalists, geologists, and engineers – as well as in medicine, secondary and higher education, and the Civil Service, where British Colonial Service officers held some 80 percent of all established posts in the Administrative grades. Even so, there was a sizeable Ghanaian commercial and professional class, with many Africans established in teaching, the Law, the Church, the Civil Service, and the liberal professions. Most important, some Ghanaians had shown keen entrepreneurial ability.

Despite these various strengths, Ghana suffered also from many weaknesses. Some of the more important of these were diagnosed by the Watson Commission.[1] Commenting on the state of the post-war economy, it considered Ghanaian agriculture to be in a very sorry state, and it admonished the colonial authorities in no uncertain terms for their failure to come to grips with the problem. 'The great majority of people', it said, 'are dependent, directly or indirectly, on agricultural production . . . Yet there was ample evidence . . . on how it was neglected' by the Government.

One of the problems faced by Ghanaian agriculture, which in 1950 accounted for almost 60 percent of GDP, is its susceptibility to changes in climatic conditions. The weather not only affects annual output and yields – which fluctuate very considerably – but also the patterns of cultivation and the regional distribution of agricultural activities. The country's two major climatic zones – distinguished by the length and intensity of the rainy season – have produced two main areas of vegetation, savanna and forest. In the savanna, the low nutrient value sub-soil and poor top-soil have always supported few crops; the major food crops being yams, groundnuts, guinea corn, and millet, and minor crops maize, rice, and tomatoes, with cattle raising also of some importance. Most of Ghana's agricultural wealth has originated in the forest zone – the main area for cocoa – with cassava and plantations as the other main crops and, of lesser importance, bananas, citrus fruits, copra, palm oil, coffee, maize and rice. In the forest zone the sub-soil is also poor, great care is required to preserve the rich top-soil, which depends for its fertility on the tree canopy. With traditional farming practice, maintaining the forest was, therefore, vital to yields.

The typical peasant farmer growing food crops – who in 1950 accounted for nearly all of Ghana's output – worked about six acres, normally divided into two or three separate units. On average, he had three times as much land in the particular area of cultivation as he actually worked; the rest lay fallow. He used little capital, and few inputs other than his and his family's labour. Under this traditional system output was limited by the time that the farmer and his family could, or wished to, devote to cultivation. Also, yields depended (weather apart) on the length of time that a piece of land could be allowed to lie fallow, and here the limit was set by population density. In the country as a whole it was not possible to provide a steady supply of food for a growing population unless new land could be brought into use. Other than the introduction of cocoa, which is not native to Ghana, there had been no innovations or changes in the first half of the century affecting traditional methods.

In 1950 just over one-third of all income from agriculture was accounted for by cocoa. Cocoa-growing provided the most important single source of cash income in the economy. Annual cocoa earnings have fluctuated widely, so that a single year's figure is misleading, but in the four years 1950–53 they accounted for just under one-fifth of total GDP and cocoa-growing provided the main form of employment for about one-fifth of the country's work force. In the same period cocoa exports accounted for 56 percent of total exports, and revenue derived from cocoa exports for 45 percent of total public revenue.

In Ghana, as in most of West Africa, cocoa has been developed as a peasant crop. Although there were many big farms in 1950, employing a considerable labour force, the typical holding has always been small, covering probably about five acres. Of the 450,000 or so people engaged in the industry in 1950, up to 300,000 were employers or heads of household farming on their own; some 100,000 more were share-croppers or paid labourers, and the rest family workers. The industry also employed large numbers of seasonal workers, many of them immigrants; the total labour force during the busiest period of the harvest usually rose to about double the number in permanent employment. The majority of cocoa farmers also cultivated food crops, with only about 60 percent of their working time spent in tending the cocoa farms and harvesting the crop. Cultivation was labour-intensive, with few purchased inputs, and relied mainly on freely available forest land. In the 1940s the crop was very remunerative, but the market was also highly volatile, with wide fluctuations in price both within the crop-year and between one crop year and the next. Also, despite the much higher overall earnings from cocoa which accrued to Ghana in the late 'forties (as compared to the early war, and immediate pre-war, periods) a big question mark hung over the future of the entire Ghanaian industry.

The main threat to supplies came from a cocoa disease known as swollen shoot, which thwarts the growth of young trees and kills mature trees. The Watson Commission estimated that in 1948 a total of 50 million trees (or about one-eighth of the total tree-stock) were affected, and that the number was increasing by 15 million a year. It warned that the cocoa industry was in danger of complete extinction in less than twenty years unless decisive action were taken. Other ills which were diagnosed included pressure on land; declining soil fertility; an inadequate rate of replanting, with a consequent ageing of the tree-stock and falling yields; the frequent mortgaging of farms which encouraged short-sighted farming practices; and the failure on the part of even the wealthier farmers to adopt techniques which would bring increased yields and lower costs. In the late 'forties world demand for cocoa seemed satisfactory, but estimates put the long-term growth in demand at no more than 3 percent per year. World output was expected to expand at a somewhat faster rate, with a depressing effect on prices. Moreover, it was feared that rapid expansion in other countries, particularly of high-yielding plantation cocoa in Latin America, would continue to make inroads into Ghana's market share even if Ghana's output could be maintained; in 1950 Ghana was still the biggest producer, accounting for a third of total world output, but its share had been declining steadily since the late 1930s.

On top of these problems, gold, manganese and diamonds – Ghana's three main mineral exports, which in 1950 accounted for almost one-quarter of total exports and generated some 5 percent of total GDP – faced an uncertain future. The mining industry was handicapped by mounting technical problems, increasingly difficult mining conditions and dwindling reserves of ore. Moreover, despite the historical importance of mining, Ghana was poorly endowed with minerals or fossil fuels. In 1950 only bauxite, which was mined in small quantities, offered opportunities for major expansion, while among known mineral deposits as yet unworked only the iron-ore deposits at Shiene were of any importance.

While more than 60 percent of GDP in 1950–53 was derived directly from agriculture and mining, only about 4 percent originated in manufacturing and public utilities. Ghana's manufacturing industry was dominated by small firms, most of which had no paid employees. In the main, manufacturing establishments were no more than primitive workshops, employing few and basic tools and little fixed capital and using craft techniques. Average output was small and often of uncertain quality, and productivity was low. Firms usually had a short life-span, and few had grown, or seemed capable of growing, much beyond the small-scale operation which the typical owner could personally control and supervise. Successful entrepreneurs tended to invest surplus funds in education, house building, or commercial ventures; diversification, rather than expansion, seemed to be the norm. Although this traditional workshop manufacturing sector was capable of supplying the basic needs – such as clothing, furniture, and household utensils – of a large section of the population, it was itself highly dependent on imported tools and materials – cloth, yarn, wire, nails, and many more items. By 1950, also, the average Ghanaian had become accustomed to many basic, but 'sophisticated', consumer goods, such as processed food, soap and detergents, cigarettes, all of which – except beer – were imported. Moreover, he was often prepared to pay a considerable premium for an imported item in preference to the – to him inferior – counterpart produced in Ghana's workshops. In 1950, the propensity to import out of additional income was very high; one estimate put the income-elasticity of consumer imports at 0.50 for urban areas, and at not much less for cocoa farmers.[2]

In the 1940s manufacturing industry had expanded rapidly, and in 1950 seemed capable of further expansion to meet the rising demand for the limited range of items that it was capable of producing. At the same time, the industry was as yet too backward to be capable of adapting quickly to supplying – against the competition of imports – the kinds of manufactures on which a growing portion of incomes was being spent.

The state of the infrastructure which served Ghana's agricultural, manufacturing, commercial, and social needs was poor, prompting some sharp criticisms from the Watson Commission. The country's transport network, for instance, which had been originally laid out in the 1920s, and had then been among the very best in Africa, had been improved only slowly; while it remained good in the African context, it had become overburdened and inadequate for Ghana's economic needs at the beginning of the 1950s.

Roads in the rural areas were poor. Many villages were several miles from the nearest country road, and this was bad at the best of times and often impassable during the rains and for months thereafter. Produce had to be head-carried for long distances, which restricted the quantity that could reach the market. This factor certainly raised costs, already inflated by the high cost of hiring lorries, which had a very short life-span on the poor roads. Transport difficulties also affected the movement of the cocoa crop. In up-country border districts communications were sometimes easier with neighbouring Togo or Ivory Coast, than with the local buying station; in such areas farmers were not slow to exploit the chance of sales across the border, with the result that the government lost cocoa revenue and the farmers began a practice of smuggling which later assumed massive proportions. The primary road network in the south, serving the main towns and mining centres – in contrast to the rural and northern road system – had been well laid; but heavy use, skimped maintenance, and unfavourable weather had all taken their toll. The lack of a proper deep water harbour in the vicinity of Accra added to the long delays in moving exports and imports, raised costs, and put still more pressure on both road and rail transport.

Besides the shortcomings of the transport system, three major deficiencies in the public services which were of direct importance to economic performance may be mentioned. First, electricity-generating capacity could not meet existing household and commercial demand. Second, water supplies, even in urban areas, were quite inadequate for household, commercial, and industrial needs. And third, health services, in respect of both personal medical care and public health, were rudimentary. While in this area Ghana was probably no worse off than other African countries, its climate made poor health a particularly severe problem. Parasitic and other debilitating diseases, most commonly malaria, bilharzia, and tuberculosis, affected large sections of the population and had a direct bearing on economic performance:

the frequent failure to harvest all of the cocoa crop, and even more notably the lime crop, may be attributed in part to the shortage of labour, which was intensified by outbreaks of disease.

Another of the criticisms of the Watson Commission was directed at Ghana's Civil Service: specifically that the administration was 'weak for the purpose of economic planning'. Its structure and philosophy prevented it, in the opinion of the Commission, from responding to the concerted pressure for economic and social improvement. At the same time the range of instruments of economic management available to the government was limited. For a start, as the Commission recognised, the almost complete lack of statistics made management difficult. There were also few credit and savings institutions which the public used. There was no Central Bank, no credit or monetary policy, no capital market, nor indeed a large business community whose behaviour monetary policy could have influenced. The Cocoa Marketing Board, which was to play an important role later, was in its infancy. Direct taxation reached only a very few people, and, with as much as 45 percent of total government revenue derived from cocoa (or 50 percent from only five export items) and a further 30 percent from imports, the usefulness of the tax system as an economic regulator was limited.

Out of Ghana's five major exports, the only one which also had an important domestic market was timber (5 percent of total exports); the other four (cocoa, gold, diamonds and manganese), accounting for 90 percent of export trade, were almost entirely dependent on outside markets. Producers thus had little scope for switching their output to the domestic market in times of low external demand or poor world prices. Since the income earned in these industries, and in activities catering for or otherwise connected with them – such as transport, commercial or other services and construction – accounted for something like 40 percent of total GDP, the fortunes of the whole economy were highly sensitive to what happened in export markets.

With Ghana's exports subject to extreme fluctuations in both price and volume, the economy was basically unstable. By building up reserves in the 1940s, the government had acquired the financial means for countering fluctuations in revenue and GDP. However, the difficulties of forecasting movements in export proceeds, overall incomes, and tax yields, made it difficult to adjust tax rates either in time or in the appropriate direction; and even if these difficulties could have been overcome, the narrow tax base reduced the impact of such measures. Given the inevitable time-lag between planning public sector projects and their execution, the obstacles to effective compensatory expenditure adjustments were formidable.

In 1950 personal savings were low in relation to income. The combined effect of low savings and high import demand was reflected in the share of consumer imports in total imports – 52 percent as against 36 percent for intermediate goods and 12 percent for capital goods. The demand for imports tended to increase particularly sharply in response to sudden changes in income, as happened between 1949–50 and 1950–51 when payments to cocoa farmers increased by 60 percent. But with traders normally holding low stocks, and long delays between the ordering and arrival of imports, increased demand tended to push up prices of imported goods. With the domestic economy also slow to respond to higher local demand, particularly for foodstuffs, sudden increases in export proceeds quickly forced up the general price level. Between 1950 and 1951, in the wake of the increase in cocoa farmer earnings, local prices of imports rose by 25 percent while their volume rose by 7 percent; the general price level also rose by 25 percent.

Despite Ghana's relatively high GDP, substantial external reserves and impressive skill endowment, the weaknesses in its economic structure – particularly the inability of food output to respond to increased demand, the inability of manufacturing to respond in those areas where demand was growing fastest, the lack of overlap between output for domestic consumption and that for export, the poor long-term prospects for Ghana's major export, the proneness of the economy to fluctuations in export earnings, and the lack of effective instruments both for regulating short-term fluctuations and for general economic management – made Ghana, in the words of Seers and Ross, 'a fragile economy'.

2. The Ten-Year Plan of 1951: the government's response to economic discontent

The period of expansion triggered by the Second World War, while giving Ghanaians a higher standard of living, also exposed the economy's many weaknesses. The war had boosted export earnings, first from minerals and later also from cocoa, in turn stimulating local demand, particularly for food and dwellings. Accra had found itself in a strategic position as a staging post for American air operations in the Mediterranean. The resulting expenditure gave rise to new employment and incomes, particularly in the construction sector, and encouraged the growth of enterprises providing a wide range of services, from repair facilities to entertainment. But in the post-war period the supply of food and other consumer goods, including imports, could not meet demand; the demand for housing and public services also outgrew supply. Prices rose quickly, with the Accra cost of living index, for example, up almost 100 percent between the end of the war and 1950. This process angered even those whose real incomes were rising. Inevitably, also, not all sections of the population could benefit from national expansion. Among them were some who were quick to voice their grievances: these included war veterans returning from overseas service, who, unwilling to go back to the land, drifted to urban areas in an often vain search for jobs and for the housing and other amenities to which army life had accustomed them; or school-leavers who were unable to find the sort of employment to which their education had encouraged them to aspire. Living standards of some groups even deteriorated; sharply, for instance, for those cocoa farmers whose trees had been ravaged by swollen-shoot disease; or for the urban unemployed, who were hardest hit by rising prices. For yet another group the war-time boom proved short-lived; the run-down of war installations, for example, was as quick in causing loss of livelihood as the original build-up had been in opening up new opportunities.

By 1947 general discontent had spilled over into active protest. A local boycott of expatriate businesses in Takoradi, in protest against alleged profiteering, quickly spread to other urban areas. By the end of the year, with the active support of organised labour and market women, it had assumed the proportions of a major challenge to authority. By early 1948 the situation had become so volatile that a single spark was capable of setting off a major explosion; and the authorities provided that spark in their reaction to a veterans' demonstration for more jobs and better pensions. This left several dead in the approaches to the Governor's Residence and provoked mass riots, looting and burning, which in turn lead to the declaration of a state of emergency and the arrest of leading African political figures, including Nkrumah.

While popular discontent posed the immediate problem of maintaining law and order, the government also faced a more fundamental challenge from sections of Ghana's educated and better-informed strata of society. Their disaffection had originated largely from political grievances, particularly after the limited response of the colonial authorities to demands for greater local autonomy. Although the then Governor, Sir Alan Burns, had in 1944 initiated a number of constitutional changes aimed at increasing African participation in government, by the end of the war the growing strength and political consciousness of the more prosperous merchant and professional classes, and the rise of a new generation of Africans educated and exposed to radical ideas abroad, brought demands for political concessions far in excess of anything Burns was prepared to support. Late in 1947 a political movement, known as the United Gold Coast Convention, or UGCC, was formed to campaign for these political demands. Early in 1948, Nkrumah, who had been abroad since before the beginning of the war, was invited to become Secretary-General of the new movement.

For the radical wing of the UGCC demands for greater political autonomy were bound up with demands for economic reform. A small ginger group, inspired by European left-wing critics of colonial economic 'exploitation' and by contemporary writings on economic growth which stressed the importance of industrialisation, as well as by the examples of India on the one hand, and the Soviet Union on the other, argued the need for greater government involvement in the economy, particularly through planning, massive programmes of education and social improvement, and a drive to set up industries and thereby reduce Ghana's dependence on the colonial power. While their views were subscribed to initially by only a minority even within the UGCC, they gained much wider currency following the Watson Commission's indictment of the government's economic measures. The Commission's comments on the precarious state of the cocoa industry, even though they were made during a healthy boom in cocoa earnings, revived an old fear, summed up in Governor Guggisberg's warning made thirty years earlier, that 'we have all our eggs in one basket . . . what if anything goes wrong with the cocoa crop or the cocoa market?'[3] The fear revealed itself, too, in a search for ways and means by which Ghana could be protected from the dangers of specialisation and dependence on one main crop. Various alternative courses of action were canvassed, from the development of new agricultural or mineral exports, to that of domestic industries and, as the most revolutionary alternative, put forward by the radical UGCC elements, the restructuring of Ghana away from the 'colonial model', for which complete independence was a prerequisite.

The colonial authorities, although slow in tackling economic problems, were not insensitive to the growing mood of frustration and discontent. In the period before discontent had turned to active protest, plans were made for major improvements in the infrastructure (including a Volta River dam), for extending educational facilities, (including the founding of the University College at Legon), and for better marketing arrangements for a number of staple food crops. In 1947 the establishment of an Industrial Development Corporation was approved. In the same year the Cocoa Marketing Board was set up, on the initiative of the Colonial office in London, to regulate the volatile cocoa market by stabilising prices to the producer, and generally to promote the well-being of the industry. Following the declaration of a state of emergency, and prompted by the criticisms of the Watson Commission, the programme of economic improvement was carried forward with more urgency. The government also announced its decision to prepare a long-term development programme; its intentions for a first phase, which was originally expected to run from April 1950 to March 1960, were outlined in a new Ten-Year Plan. But the Plan was actually launched in January 1951, less than two months before the elections which brought Nkrumah into government, and which set Ghana on the road to complete independence six years later.

In view of Nkrumah's critical attitude towards colonial economic policy, his election victory threatened to kill the Plan at birth. The planners had not anticipated this outcome to the elections, but they had made provision for periodic revisions in the light of changing economic circumstances. In the event these, starting with a major revision in 1952, incorporated in part the new post-election economic philosophy, and the Plan survived formally until independence in March 1957. But despite the short life of the Plan in its original form, it is important to note its major provisions because Nkrumah's own programme was partly a reaction to them; at the same time other provisions remained substantially unchanged, and the planning techniques also survived into the post-independence period.

The original Ten-Year Plan was, in essence, little more than a declaration of intent in respect of the level of public investment and its distribution among various ministries. It envisaged total government investment of £7.4m. a year over the decade; a 20 percent increase over the level of government capital spending during 1947–50. The proposed level of investment does not now appear ambitious. But its appropriateness to the circumstances of the 1950s was difficult to judge without reference to a macro-economic framework, or quantitative targets for national income and its main component parts; and these could not be prepared in 1950 on the then available statistics and information. In setting the level of investment, the government was guided, in effect, by its particular assessment of four main factors:

availability of finance; the right balance between the public and private sectors; the economy's ability to absorb additional public investment spending; and the implementing capacity of the government machine itself.

In view of the government's dependence for its revenue on cocoa, whose supply position was uncertain and for which the world market was notoriously difficult to forecast, there was a predisposition to play safe and set a modest level. The Plan estimated that 62 percent of the public investment programme of £74m. could be financed from Ghana's resources: 17 percent from recurrent budget surpluses; 35 percent from duty on additional cocoa export proceeds; and 10 percent from reserves held by the Cocoa Marketing Board. The balance was to be made up by British aid funds (5 percent of the Plan total) and by borrowing (33 percent), mainly from abroad. Thus, even with an 'unambitious' investment programme, the planned external financing need, at £28m., was substantial. However, the government had reserves on which to fall back in case it could not raise this amount. Its own reserves in 1950 stood at £10m. (excluding those tied up in pension or sinking funds). In addition, a part of the £52m. held by the Cocoa Marketing Board and the £32m. by the West African Currency Board could be mobilised. Ghana's resources were, therefore, not as modest as the government suggested.

Even so, since the public sector had to make provisions for investments in education, health, security, infrastructure and so on, many of which by their very nature could bring no quick economic return and therefore no substantial new sources of revenue, the government was anxious not to allow the rate of increase in public investment to rise above that of output in the private sector. Its own assessment of the private sector's potential for rapid expansion in the early 1950s was pessimistic. This was reinforced by the view that, while government could encourage the private sector by the provision of public services and by other measures, the essentially spontaneous nature of the development process made such measures useful only within narrow limits. At the same time the government was concerned that a rapid increase in public spending, even if it could be financed, would overtax capacity in the construction industry, and, given the difficulties already experienced in obtaining materials and other essential imported equipment, would only exacerbate the shortages and force up prices.

Total investment under the Plan was to be distributed between four broad categories, as follows: 17 percent for 'economic and productive services' (including agriculture, industry, electricity, and water); 35 percent for 'communications' (road, rail, harbour, and telecommunications); 33 percent for 'social services' (education, health, housing, and welfare); and 15 percent for 'common services and general administration' (government offices, police and prisons, defence, etc).

In allocating public investment funds between different ministries and different sectors, the government claimed to have followed two main guiding principles. The first was to avoid 'undue bias towards any particular aspect of development'.[4] In the context of the then current debate on economic policy, and considered in conjunction with other evidence from the Plan, this observation must be taken as a rejection of demands that the government should bring about major structural changes in the economy. It preferred to aim at strengthening the major weak points in the existing structure, and at supporting those sectors which offered the best chance of an immediate economic return. This is made explicit in the second guiding principle of the Plan: 'pride of place', it stated, was to be given to 'economic and productive services, with particular attention to agriculture in its widest sense, to industry and to water supplies on which so much depends'.[5]

Against this declared priority, the allocation of only 17 percent of total public investment to projects which, in terms of the government's own definition, were considered 'productive', appears meagre. But the Plan figures refer only to public spending, and the government looked to the private sector, domestic and expatriate, to provide the bulk of investment in both agriculture and industry. Its own spending plans for these sectors were confined to advisory and support services, such as geological and hydrological surveys, research, experimental crop production, disease control, extension facilities; industrial and agricultural credit; and marketing. Most required only small capital outlays compared with those needed for, say, major infrastructure schemes. And investment in the latter inevitably had to come mainly from the public sector.

The question of the productivity of public investment – in this and subsequent plans – will be taken up again later. At this stage, it should be noted that the government's own classification, in which entire categories of capital spending were designated as 'productive' and others as 'unproductive' or 'social' was extremely crude – a factor which assumed considerable importance during the Nkrumah period. Under the classification in the Ten-Year-Plan, a capital item was deemed to be 'productive' if it promoted directly the output of goods and services for the market. In practice, because of the difficulty of defining what was meant by 'directly', any capital item which was carried in the Estimates of departments responsible for agriculture, mining, industry, and commerce came to be classed as 'productive'. The classification made no allowance for the fact that some 'social' spending, (to take an example from the Plan, the purchase of equipment for preventive spraying against malaria) could yield economic returns commensurate with those obtained from 'productive' investments (such as the installation of electricity generating capacity, or the purchase of tractors). Moreover, it made no distinction between the time over which the economic returns on a project accrued. Since, for example, all agricultural investment was classified as productive, it blurred the difference between the purchase of a tractor, where the capital cost might be 'recovered' through increased output in five years, and the setting up of an agricultural research station, where the capital cost might be 'recovered' in not less than ten years. The crudeness of this classification of public investment had no great practical significance as long as those who used it understood its shortcomings. However, after 1951, with less experienced leaders gaining an increasingly influential voice in economic policy, these shortcomings tended to be overlooked, and the classification came to be used as a guide to public investment in a way which could only mislead.

3. The evolution of Nkrumah's economic programme for independence.

Until Nkrumah's return to Ghana in early 1948, the drive for greater local autonomy, spearheaded by the intelligentsia represented in the UGCC and the economic protest movement of the masses, had followed separate paths. The arrest of the UGCC leaders after the riots sparked off by the veterans' protest march offered a common cause in which the two movements could have united against the authorities. But the main body of the UGCC was quick to dissociate itself from the violence of the popular protest movement, and to agree to co-operate with the authorities in working out new constitutional arrangements for a greater degree of local autonomy. Nkrumah, in contrast, exploited the sudden popular acclaim his arrest had offered: he organised a splinter group of the UGCC into a new political party (Peoples' Convention Party or CPP), boycotted the work of the constitutional committee under Coussey[6] on the grounds that it represented only the views of the privileged sections of the community, and launched his mass campaign of 'positive action' for immediate self-rule. Later, he modified his view and decided that the CCP should, after all, contest the 1951 elections to be held under the new Coussey Constitution, even though its provisions came well short of self-rule; and, having won the elections, he accepted the post of Leader of Government Business, and, in 1952, the newly-created office of Prime Minister.

On taking office, Nkrumah's position was not easy. His political power was based on the support of two main groups: the discontented urban masses, and the equally discontented 'half-privileged' – artisans, clerical workers, school leavers, junior Civil Servants, primary school teachers, and market women. Both groups were volatile and their support could prove ephemeral. By his quarrel with the main body of the UGCC, and the campaign of demonstrations and civil disobedience, Nkrumah had already alienated the merchant and professional classes, including many Africans in the higher reaches of the Civil Service, as well as the traditional Chiefs. By accepting office, and with it implicitly the provisions of the Ten-Year Plan, he disillusioned also the more radical among his educated CPP supporters. At the same time, the ultimate executive power remained vested in the Governor, the important portfolios of Finance, Justice and External Affairs in the hands of Colonial Service Officers, and the Civil Service largely expatriate. Since neither Nkrumah nor his senior African colleagues had had any previous experience of government, they needed time to find their feet. Moreover, they were anxious to show that Africans in government could be responsible, and to avoid doing anything which would prejudice the move towards full political independence.

Nkrumah had also come to office without any clear idea of the economic strategy he might pursue in preference to that laid down in the Ten-Year Plan. He therefore had no real alternative to going along with the policy of the government as already laid down. Apart from implementing the Plan the government's most pressing priority at the time was to carry out a major cocoa rehabilitation programme; Nkrumah's first important act in office in the economic field was to put his authority and effort behind this programme, with notable success.

By early 1952 he became frustrated with what seemed to him unjustifiably slow progress in implementing the public investment provisions of the Ten-Year Plan, and worried by possible disaffection among his supporters. Before the elections he had stressed that no major economic improvements could be expected until independence had been achieved – a philosophy summed up in his slogan 'seek ye first the political kingdom, and all things will be added to it'. Once in office he did not feel confident of keeping the support of the masses unless the government with which he was identified could begin to meet the demand for jobs, for better urban conditions, for a steady supply of food and other consumer staples, and for adequate imports at 'fair' prices. Besides, he was anxious to tackle the job of transforming Ghana into a 'modern' state – with its roads, harbours, schools, hospitals, power stations, mechanised farms and factories – all of which he considered that Ghana lacked largely through colonial negligence.

In the course of 1952 Nkrumah succeeded in getting the government to agree that the Ten-Year Plan should be implemented in five years, that is by the end of 1955 rather than 1960. In the same year the Plan was also expanded by the addition of projects originally included in outline form in a 'reverse plan'. Thus, within eighteen months of the launching of the Ten-Year Plan, the earlier policy which emphasised caution was entirely reversed.

While the pressure which Nkrumah and his African colleagues could exert from within the Cabinet was one crucial element in this turn-about, three other specific factors also affected both its nature and timing. First, it had become evident that the capacity of ministries to prepare and execute projects had been underestimated when the Plan outline was settled in 1950. Second, the revenue outlook appeared brighter. The effect of these two factors was reinforced by the third, the authoritative reappraisal of Ghana's economic problems made by the Seers-Ross economic mission sent from the Colonial Office in London. Seers and Ross had come to Ghana to investigate what constraints, if any, the building and construction industry imposed on development and, more generally, whether there were serious inflationary implications in an expanded public investment programme. In their 1952 report, they concluded that the immediate causes of inflationary pressure and economic instability, in conditions of low supply elasticity of domestic consumer goods output and of physical limitations on the supply of imports, were the rapid growth and instability of cocoa incomes. They concluded, also, that the terms of reference of the Cocoa Marketing Board (CMB) required it to pursue a policy which helped to exacerbate instability: by trying to stabilise prices to farmers from year to year, while output fluctuated widely, the Board helped to destabilise cocoa incomes, and thereby also aggregate income, and in turn, demand for consumer goods, imports, prices and finally wages. Overall stability would be easier to maintain, they thought, by stabilising cocoa farmer *incomes* rather than prices. Seers and Ross also found that cocoa farmers spent a large part of their income on consumer imports or dwellings, and that they therefore placed a particularly severe strain on the building industry, on the available supply of materials, and on the country's capacity to handle and distribute imports. The most expedient course for relieving pressure in all these areas, and making room for more public investment spending, they argued, was to restrict for the time being CMB payments to cocoa farmers.[7]

As the CMB had a buying and exporting monopoly, the government had the administrative means for restraining cocoa incomes. The Board had already set the precedent of fixing the producer price paid to farmers well below the world export price so as to be able to accumulate a reserve for discharging its statutory obligation to support prices during periods of slump. It was a relatively easy matter to maintain the price at a level which would direct additional proceeds from exports into the public treasury. The average producer price paid since the CMB's establishment in 1947 was already almost double that to which the farmers had become accustomed before 1947; there was, therefore, no real urgency for allowing it to rise much higher, even if export prices improved still further. The diversion of additional cocoa export proceeds away from cocoa farmers could swell public revenue substantially and, at the same time, increase the economy's capacity to absorb additional public investment.

Seers and Ross had thus shown that the effective choice, provided that cocoa prices did not plunge from the new post-war plateau, lay not between more or less public investment, but between a higher level of public investment and a higher level of cocoa farmer consumption. When the alternatives were presented in these terms, the expatriate members of the government felt unable to reject African demands for a more ambitious public investment effort.

The CPP's election victory had in the meantime also helped to reopen the case for economic 'restructuring' which the Ten-Year Plan strategy had rejected. As a first gambit, Nkrumah invited the eminent economist Arthur Lewis to report on the potential for industrialisation and its likely contribution to future development. Seers and Ross had already prepared the ground by arguing that Ghana's problems of instability and recurring inflation could be tackled by a planned diversification of exports away from cocoa, and by 'restructuring' – i.e. engineering a closer balance between the structure of domestic output and of domestic demand. The government had accepted this view in 1952, if only implicitly, in its decision to divert further sums from cocoa earnings to finance investment in other sectors. What still remained to be settled was the future sectoral allocation of these funds.

Seers and Ross had themselves backed more investment in infrastructure and in agriculture, both for export and for domestic consumption, which coincided broadly with the declared priorities in the original Ten-Year Plan. Lewis took up a similar position. 'The number one priority', he thought, 'is a concentrated attack on the system of growing food'.[8] Also, the government could promote development 'by spending its money on expanding the public services', which he considered 'woefully inadequate'. Referring to industry, he ruled out the possibility of an early development of manufactures for export, but considered that the manufacture of commodities for the home market deserved support, although 'a major programme in this sphere should wait'. Lewis recommended, therefore, a modest programme of state encouragement to industry. He proposed reform and strengthening of the Industrial Development Corporation and advised that some funds should be set aside for investment in joint enterprises, in industrial estates, and in a limited number of state factories with 'pioneering' or public utility status. Beyond that the government should not go: in any case, foreign private enterprise should be looked to as the main source of funds and technical expertise for industrial development.

These recommendations were accepted; and in subsequent Plan revisions no new public funds were allotted for industry over and above those provided in the original Plan. Nevertheless proponents of industrialisation did not feel that Lewis had closed the door on Ghanaian industrialisation, but that he had merely advised its postponement. They attached great significance to his observation that improvements in the infrastructure and in public services would reduce the cost of manufacturing, which would 'automatically attract new industries, without the government having to offer special favours'.[9] In supporting a greater effort in infrastructure and education, Nkrumah and others therefore felt that they were laying the foundations on which industry would rise in the future; and the greater the effort made in laying these foundations, the shorter the time in which industrial ambitions would be realised.

The original Ten-Year Plan had not been able to provide a clear set of national priorities or to point Ghana towards any particular long-term objective. A policy of restructuring and diversification, as understood by Seers and Ross, provided the Plan with the sense of purpose or direction that was missing and the means for a clearer ordering of Ghana's economic priorities. The measures they implied seemed appropriate for giving Ghana faster and more solidly based growth. However, there is no evidence that Nkrumah had more than a hazy understanding of what was involved. His own writings suggest that he had a good grasp of Ghana's major economic weaknesses; but they suggest, equally, that his conception of the industrial Ghana to which he aspired was vague. He had before him, as models, the rich, industrial societies of Britain and America, but there is no evidence that he had any real understanding of how their economies worked, and what it had taken to create them. He appeared incapable of conceiving any intermediate position between the Ghana he knew and the industrial countries which he knew, nor did he question Ghana's capacity to engineer, in time, its transformation from its current state to one resembling Britain or America. For Nkrumah, therefore, restructuring was not so much a strategy as an objective; which could be advanced by the simple device of spending money on roads, harbours, power stations, schools, and such like, which would, in turn, bring industrial, commercial, and agricultural development.

From 1953 onwards Nkrumah's hopes for transforming Ghana into a 'modern state' thus rested firmly on a massive public investment effort, concentrating on infrastructure, public services, and education. In line with this view, and in the wake of the post-Korean War boom in cocoa prices, total planned investment was enlarged at each annual revision, reaching its zenith in the revision for 1955, made in late 1954, only months after Ghana had attained full internal self-government. By 1955 planned investment had grown from the original £74m. over ten years, to £122m. over five years (with £66m. actually spent). Despite this increase, the revenue situation by 1954 had improved so considerably since the original Plan was prepared that the government was able to reduce the planned external loan requirement from £23m. (or 33 percent of the original total) to £12m. (or 10 percent of the larger total).[10]

Changes in the main categories of investment in the Plan between 1951 and 1955 are summarised in Table 2.1. These in part reflect alterations in project preparation capacity of different ministries, unconnected with staffing changes made in line with reappraised priorities. These alterations explain the smaller shares of investment in the revised Plan allocated to the so-called 'productive' sectors of agriculture and industry – although these shares were also automatically lowered by the big increase in the allocation to 'General Government'. But the greater relative and absolute emphasis given to infrastructure and to education (as opposed to other 'social' sectors)

Table 2.1 Planned distribution of public investment under the Ten-Year Plan

Sector[1]	Original Plan as published (£m)	(%)	Revised Plan as at 31.12.1955 (£m)	(%)
Agriculture	4.2	(6)	6.0	(5)
Manufacturing & Mining	4.4	(6)	3.5	(3)
Infrastructure & Public Services	29.1	(40)	55.5	(45)
Education	12.3	(16)	13.4	(10)
Health, Social Services & Housing	13.0	(17)	12.9	(11)
General Government[2]	11.0	(15)	30.0	(25)
Total	74.0	(100)	121.5	(100)

Notes: 1. Investments here classified as 'Agriculture' and 'Manufacturing and Mining' were included in the original Plan under 'Economic and productive services'. This category included also electricity, included here under 'Infrastructure and Public Services', and water supplies, included here partly under 'Infrastructure and Public Services', and partly under 'Health, Social Services and Housing'.

2. Includes public buildings (with equipment); general services, e.g. justice, information; capital grants to local government; etc.

Sources: **Ten-Year Plan**
Economic Survey 1955 (Appendix, Table 15)
Economic Survey 1957 (Supplementary Tables)

does reflect the new concern with the idea of 'restructuring', as understood by Nkrumah. However, apart from these changes of emphasis between broad categories of investment, the investment programme retained much the same character as before 1951. Individual investments continued to reflect the sectoral or sub-sectoral objectives of the different ministries as they saw them; and the separate

Table 2.2 Proposed sources of finance for the Ten-Year Plan

<table>
<tr><th rowspan="2">Source of finance</th><th colspan="2">Original Plan Estimates</th><th colspan="2">Revised estimates as at 31.12.1955</th></tr>
<tr><th>(£m)</th><th>(%)</th><th>(£m)</th><th>(%)</th></tr>
<tr><td>Current budget surpluses</td><td>13.1</td><td>(17)</td><td>19.7</td><td>(16)</td></tr>
<tr><td>Additional cocoa revenue</td><td>26.5</td><td>(35)</td><td>73.8</td><td>(61)</td></tr>
<tr><td>Cocoa Marketing Board loans</td><td>7.5</td><td>(10)</td><td>6.9</td><td>(6)</td></tr>
<tr><td>Official aid</td><td>3.0[1]</td><td>(4)</td><td>3.7[2]</td><td>(3)</td></tr>
<tr><td>Miscellaneous overseas</td><td>0.8[3]</td><td>(1)</td><td>2.5[4]</td><td>(2)</td></tr>
<tr><td>Local loans</td><td rowspan="2">23.0[5]</td><td rowspan="2">(33)</td><td>2.5</td><td>(2)</td></tr>
<tr><td>Foreign loans</td><td>12.4[6]</td><td>(10)</td></tr>
<tr><td>Total</td><td>74.0</td><td>(100)</td><td>121.5</td><td>(100)</td></tr>
</table>

Notes:
1. British Colonial Development and Welfare Funds, unused portion remaining by January 1951, out of ten-year allocation of £3.5m. made in 1945.
2. As note 1; plus £0.2m, British contribution to the Volta Project Preparatory Commission; plus £0.5m, in US aid from Marshal Plan allocation to Britain.
3. Repayment of war-loan made to Britain.
4. As note 3; plus interest receipts on Ghana Government investments in Sterling securities (£1.6m.); plus other minor items.
5. Mainly foreign loans.
6. Residual item.

Sources: Ten-Year Plan
Economic Survey, 1955, Table 33.

programmes of different ministries were not yet reshaped and integrated into a new strategy; there is no evidence that the 'restructuring' idea had yet been translated into an actual strategy.

The policy of development and restructuring through large-scale public investment in infrastructure, basic services, and education ran into trouble as early as mid-1955. Between 1950 and the end of 1954 the rapid increase in central government spending – 250 percent on capital account and over 300 percent on recurrent account – still lagged behind the increase in public revenue, and the government was able to add £55m. to its reserves. The balance of payments, too, was strong, and £77m. was added to external reserves. In 1954, in response to an unprecedented upsurge in revenue (from £44m. in 1953 to £68m.) further big additions to planned public investment were made. The revenue upsurge, however, proved short-lived; revenue fell sharply in 1955 and again in 1956, and by 1957 it was back to the 1953 level of £44m. In the meantime, budget spending continued to rise. A large number of projects had been started or contracted in 1953 and 1954. Moreover, projects being completed made new demands on the recurrent budget, to cover operating expenses, purchase of materials, and payments to staff. By the second half of 1955 the budget had moved into deficit. Ghana's highest ever surplus in 1954 (of £24m.) was followed by another surplus, of £10m. in 1955, but then by deficits of £9m. in 1956 and £10m. in 1957. In these same two years the balance of payments was also in deficit, for the first time since before the war, and external reserves had to be drawn on to the tune of £37m.

The appearance of budgetary and balance of payments deficits provided those who had been reluctantly drawn into accepting Nkrumah's policies with an opportunity to reassert themselves. The Ministry of Finance, in particular, was anxious to see deficits brought quickly under control, preferably by cuts in public spending. It deplored especially what it described as the trend towards a 'preponderance of investment in public buildings and social services and the relatively small investment in enterprises likely to provide an expanding source of revenue'.[11] This view was in keeping with its traditional insistence that public spending should not be allowed to get out of line with progress in the private sector. And precisely this seemed to be happening: preliminary estimates for 1956 showed that private fixed capital formation rose by about 75 percent between 1950 and 1956, only about half the rise witnessed in the public sector; that GDP fell in 1955 and again in 1956; and that cocoa output, still the revenue mainstay, continued to stagnate at about its 1951 level.

In the two years before independence the available evidence thus appeared to suggest that Nkrumah's policies were failing, and that the conservative view, which had dominated before 1952, had been vindicated after all. But the situation was in reality not all that bad, as later evidence showed.[12] In the first place, revised estimates showed that fixed capital formation in the private sector between 1950 and

1956 had risen almost as quickly as in the public sector; in 1956 the private share in the total came to about 67 percent as against 71 percent in 1950. GDP, rather than falling in 1955 and 1956, had risen by a total 20 percent in real terms. Cocoa output had been stagnant, but – as scheduled – the rehabilitation and replanting campaign of 1951 began to bear fruit handsomely from about 1958 on. External reserves, despite the trade deficit in 1956, had increased by some £77m. since 1950, to £190m. at the end of 1956. And, finally, inflation – which had been such a persistent problem since the war – had been brought completely under control after 1951.

While the budget deficits which first appeared in the second half of 1955 can be formally attributed to 'overspending', it is clear that they were partly due to the government's inability to tap an expanding source of revenue – which cuts in spending would not solve. Moreover, after the unusually large surplus in 1954, there was no reason why the Ghana government should not have considered using, as a matter of course, a part of this surplus to sustain a somewhat higher rate of investment than could be financed from revenue over the next few years, particularly in view of its substantial reserves. In calling in 1956 for an immediate effort to restore budgetary balance by cuts in spending the Ministry of Finance thus seems, in retrospect, to have acted in an unnecessarily alarmist manner.

However, the Ministry's warning on the trend towards 'unproductive' investments was timely. Even though its case rested partly on misleading statistics, and partly on a crude distinction between 'productive' and 'unproductive' investments, it rightly challenged the belief that there was an inevitable connection between public spending on infrastructure or public services and economic growth. While the information then available made it impossible to assess the 'productivity' of Ghana's public investment as a whole, it became clear later that the rise in private sector investment and activity (as recorded in the revised GDP estimates) was stimulated mainly by new demand created by the spate of government contracts and general spending, and to only a small extent by improvements which directly affected private sector productivity or production costs. (Among the few investments with the latter effect one may include the measures to improve food storage in the north of Ghana; the construction of new cocoa buying stations; some of the improvements in water supply and electricity distribution; some of the investments of the Industrial Development Corporation; miscellaneous improvements in public services – government workshops, vocational training centres, government transport etc; and, most important, a number of projects in the transport field intended to clear particularly severe bottlenecks, affecting mainly the movement of bulky exports and imports.) If Ghana allowed itself to settle into a pattern of demand-led growth, financed by the budget deficits, there was the real danger that it would not be able to change course in the future without a major contraction in private sector incomes and employment.

Nkrumah's reaction to the deficits was one of disappointment that after six years of heavy public investment on modernising the infrastructure and the public services there should be so little evidence of local investment in the 'modern' industries he had hoped to see, or of interest from potential overseas investors. But since his main concern at the time was with preparations for independence, he was anxious not to arouse further accusations of mismanagement or irresponsibility, which might have prejudiced Ghana's independence time-table. He thus accepted, if reluctantly, the need for temporary public investment restraint to bring the budget and balance of payments deficits under control. By independence, public investment had lost momentum, and this provided a suitable opportunity for formally abandoning the Colonial Ten-Year Plan and pausing for a period of 'consolidation' during which the choices facing Ghana could be considered and new policies for independence worked out.

4. Aid and foreign private investment up to independence

In the original Ten-Year Plan it was envisaged that a third of public sector investment would have to be financed from overseas grants and loans (see Table 2.2). The investment targets did not include, of course, the private sector, so there is no figure for expected contributions from overseas investors; it was nevertheless assumed that investment finance for the needs of the mining industry would be raised overseas, that foreign companies engaged in general trading, construction, timber, and services would provide some of their investment finance from abroad, and that some new capital could be attracted into manufacturing ventures.

When the Ten-Year Plan was launched in 1951, only £2.7m. had been secured out of the required overseas contribution of £26m. in grants and loans to the public sector. The money came entirely from British Colonial Development and Welfare Funds (CD&W), which then provided the major source of British government capital aid to the colonies. The £2.7m. available was the balance remaining from the 1945 allocation of £3.5m., which had been intended for the ten-year period from 1954–5. The estimates of foreign borrowing and aid for the Plan were made on the assumption that colonial status would continue; this assumption was, however, invalidated almost at once with the result that Ghana's access to British public funds substantially changed. A new allocation was originally expected for 1955 onwards, but by then it was clear that Ghana was nearing full independence, after which date it would no longer qualify for CD&W money; and, moreover, it would lose the preferential access to the London capital market which colonies enjoyed through Trustee Stock status which, among other advantages, conferred British government guarantees on their loan issues. However, until March 1957, while Ghana formally remained a British colony, its opportunities for approaching other potential donors were limited. Only the World Bank, and to a lesser extent the United States, were willing to contemplate giving aid, through Britain as the metropolitan power. In the event, largely as a result of the post-Korean war boom cocoa prices, Ghana was able to get by without new capital from public sources overseas.

Partly for this reason, and partly because of his interest in obtaining the skills, experience, and know-how for industrial development, Nkrumah's main concern in the period up to independence was with direct private foreign investment. His first public appeal for investment capital and technical help was made in 1951 to the Black community in America. In making this appeal Nkrumah came out against the view of many of his radical CPP supporters who, while being the most ardent supporters of industrial development, opposed foreign investment on the grounds that it would perpetuate Ghana's 'colonial' dependence. Opposition to foreign investment had become sufficiently vocal for Lewis to warn that 'there is no question that industrialisation is impossible in (Ghana) without bringing in the knowledge of expatriates; . . . if the Government were determined to exclude private capital it would be better to postpone industrialisation.'

It is difficult to gauge the effect of this controversy on actual investment decisions; but the fierce attacks from some sections of the CPP must have added to the general feeling of uncertainty which the CPP's election victory had already induced. In the 1940s private investment from overseas had been a mere trickle; in 1951 there was what amounted to a minor panic, with a recorded private long-term outflow of almost £11m. But the panic was short-lived; already in 1953 the balance of payments accounts record an inflow of over £6m., and a steady, if unspectacular, inflow continued until 1956; but then it was followed by a small outflow over the next three years. It is possible that the Lewis Report had some part in helping to restore confidence in 1953, particularly in view of Nkrumah's known support. As he declared later, 'it would be many years before (Ghana) would be in a position to find from its own resources people who could combine capital with the experience required in the development and management of new industries and the country would therefore have to rely to a large extent on foreign enterprise.' Nkrumah made it clear that foreign capital investment in industry would be encouraged and, moreover, that Ghana would be prepared to offer financial grants and other forms of help to companies willing to establish large-scale enterprises. The main reservation to the 'open-door' policy concerned the government's right to insist on partnership where its 'participation was calculated to serve the national interest'. An additional, and reasonable, qualification was laid down to the effect that overseas investors had a responsibility for training local personnel: 'whilst we appreciated that in industry the criterion must be that of industrial efficiency, the warmth of our welcome to both publicly and privately owned enterprises would depend on the extent to which they provided for the training of African employees for eventual employment in senior technical, professional and managerial appointments.' Probably still more reassuring than Nkrumah's stand was the fact that the arrival of internal self-government in 1954 had not brought any obvious worsening in the climate in which foreign enterprises operated, nor any deliberately discriminatory government measures. But as Britain still exercised some general supervision of government, uncertainty remained on the position after independence; this may have accounted for the slight outflow of capital just before and after independence.

While the balance of payments figures appear to show that the political climate had a direct effect on private long-term capital flows, the recorded ups and downs in the flow are also consistent with fluctuations in Ghana's GDP; the peak for capital inflows coincided with a period of rapid expansion (1953–6), and capital outflow with periods of stagnation or contraction (1950–2 and again 1957–8). It would be dangerous, however, to infer too much from the figures themselves: annual flows were small, so that one or two decisions, possibly affected by considerations which had no immediate connection with events in Ghana, could make nonsense of any apparently neat pattern. Smaller companies appear to have been sensitive to short-term economic and political developments; this applied to some extent also to companies without previous experience of Ghana, but which became interested possibly as a result of the incentives which were promised. But the larger expatriate companies which dominated the 'modern' mining, industrial and commercial life of Ghana – such as the United Africa Group, CAST (diamonds), and Barclays DCO – planned on the basis of longer-term political and economic prospects, within a wider framework of their other international interests. Moreover, the timing of their investments, and the sources from which they were financed, were affected as much by internal company considerations as by current Ghanaian events.

Traditionally, foreign private investment in Ghana had gone into mining and commerce (importing, exporting, wholesale and general trading, and financial service). To a lesser extent, it had also been attracted into the construction and timber industries. In the 1950s, the mining sector offered few new opportunities for investment[14] but timber and construction attracted some foreign capital, encouraged in the latter directly by the boom in public works and building. Investment in foreign-owned commercial concerns, particularly in the form of buildings (banks, shops, service stations) also experienced a minor boom, especially after 1954. For the government, however, the main attraction of foreign investment lay in its potential contribution to the development of manufacturing industries; but it was also in this field that Ghana's attractions to the foreign investor were least.

In tropical Africa generally only a very small proportion of foreign investment had gone into manufacturing industries. Ghana was thus asking investors to break new ground just at a time when Africa's relative attraction was declining. In the first place, the progressive relaxation of restrictions on capital export from Britain (the major source of capital for Sterling Area Africa) made it easier to invest British capital outside the Sterling Area. While this did not affect the traditional areas of investment, such as mining, it helped to divert elsewhere new capital which might have looked for an outlet in African manufacturing industries. Even more important, perhaps, were economic and technological developments in the industrial world itself, which encouraged both the retention of capital for expanding capital-intensive industries at home, and its export to other developed countries in preference to developing countries in general. Finally, there was little in the way of local manufacturing industry in Africa to provide a base for newcomers.

No more than half a dozen of the expatriate companies operating in Ghana were engaged in manufacturing; there were only limited prospects, therefore, that industrial development would be based on the activities of companies which were already established locally. Of the expatriate companies which were engaged in timber, construction, distribution, and trading, some had the resources and know-how for diversifying into manufacturing; some did diversify into simple manufacturing activities (such as from saw-milling into plywood); others into local finishing and packaging of imports (e.g. soft drinks bottling). In 1952 Lewis had identified only limited possibilities for expanding local manufacture,[15] and little had changed by the time of independence. The investor who had funds to put into one of the 'favourable' areas listed in the Lewis Report still had to face formidable production and marketing problems; lack of a local industrial tradition, with few local industries which could supply his need for semi-manufactured inputs, and no pool of skilled staff that he could tap; an uncertain supply of raw materials; and a small, virtually unprotected, market, with very strong brand-loyalty for existing products, a high status-value attached to imports, and competition from entrenched expatriate companies engaged in the local distribution of imports.

The government hoped to compensate for some of these disadvantages by offering cash grants, help in the acquisition and preparation of suitable industrial sites and staff housing, and priority in the provision of public services, including water, power, access roads, special dock facilities and telecommunications. But the value of these 'incentives' was largely offset by the inefficiency with which the Industrial Development Corporation and the Industries Section in the Ministry of Commerce handled overseas enquiries. They were fore instance, slow in following up expressions of interest; partly, this was due to the chronic shortage of staff with the required skills and experience. Despite the government's interest in private foreign investment, there was, in effect, a general lack of urgency to seek out potential investors and to follow up, as a matter of priority, expressions of interest which offered real prospects. This general lack of urgency contrasted sharply with the determination and persistence shown later in promoting foreign participation in the Volta Project (see Chapter 3) and ultimately it prevented the Volta Project from itself stimulating other private foreign investment.

During the life of the Ten-Year Plan, then, from January 1951 to June 1957, net aid and foreign investment in Ghana amounted to only £3.5m. and £7.0m. respectively, making a total external contribution of £10.5m. Over the same period Ghana financed out of its own resources domestic capital expenditure (private and public) amounting to some

£350m.; and, moreover, it invested another £57m. net in sterling securities out of its substantial overall trading surplus. The country was thus not only financially self-reliant, but also an important creditor in its own right. Within four years of independence, however, the position was reversed.

Notes

1. Three-man Commission set up in 1948 under the chairmanship of A. Watson, K.C, to 'enquire into and report on the recent disturbances . . . and the underlying causes'.
2. Quoted by D. Seers and C. Ross, *Financial and Physical Problems of Development in the Gold Coast*, Government Printer, Accra, 1952.
3. Legislation Council address, 1919.
4. *Ten-Year Plan of Development and Welfare*, Introduction.
5. ibid.
6. The Coussey Commission was set up after the 1948 disorders, to study the new constitution.
7. The academic controversy surrounding the policies of West African Marketing Boards remains a *cause célèbre*. For the opposing view to that put forward by Seers and Ross, see Peter Bauer, *West African Trade*, Routledge & Kagan Paul, London (reissued 1963), Section 5.
8. *Report on Industrialisation and the Gold Coast*, A. Lewis, Government Printer, Accra, 1953.
9. ibid.
10. See Table 2.2.
11. *Economic Survey*, 1955, p. 21 (published in 1956).
12. Ghana's National Income Accounts were revised with UN assistance in 1961–62. See Appendix note on Ghana's statistics and note on sources for Table A.2.
13. Speech in the Legislative Assembly, 1 March 1954.
14. See above, Section 1.
15. Vegetable oils, canned fruit and vegetables, salt, beer, bricks and tiles, cement, glass, lime juice, industrial alcohol, wood products and miscellaneous chemicals.

Chapter 3 The Transition from Financial Self-reliance to External Dependence (1957–1961)

1. Preparations for Ghana's first post-independence Plan

Work on a new plan, to replace the discarded Ten-Year Plan, started within a few months of independence (in March 1957). The new plan was to be launched in 1959; in the meantime, from July 1957 to June 1959, there was to be a period of 'consolidation' during which it was planned to complete projects under way and the more urgent projects from the discarded Ten-Year Plan which were already in an advanced state of preparation. It was hoped, too, that by the time the new plan was ready, budgetary and balance of payments stability would have been secured, and new contacts with potential economic partners abroad established.

The main responsibility for preparing a plan strategy and co-ordinating the work of different government departments was entrusted, as for the Ten-Year Plan, to a Standing Development Committee composed of senior ministers, now under the chairmanship of Nkrumah. The Committee was to be serviced by a Development Secretariat staffed largely by administrative officers. The former was to be concerned mainly with the political guidelines and overall objectives of the plan, while the latter was to undertake most of the detailed work of planning, project selection and so on. The government also obtained the services of Arthur Lewis to help with the preparatory work.

The membership of the Development Committee and the Secretariat represented, though not without some overlap, two different view-points; these perpetuated, in a formal structure, the old differences between the conservative policies of the Colonial Service Officers, and the expansionist ambitions of Nkrumah and many of his African political colleagues. The broad consensus of the Secretariat – the planners – supported by the Ministry of Finance and the newly founded Bank of Ghana, was against a rapid expansion of public investment and against the financing of investment out of accumulated reserves. The Committee – or politicians – on the other hand, saw in the high level of public investment a necessary condition for vigorous growth; they considered it also an important political requirement. For most of them, the accumulated reserves were there to be used.

Detailed work on the new Five-Year Plan started on the basis of a compromise which reflected rather more closely the view of the planners. The preliminary guidelines for the capital budget for the new plan, issued to ministries in December 1957[1], envisaged an overall level of public investment of between £80m. and £100m. (at 1957 prices) over five years, or between £16m. and £20m. a year. This compared with an average annual rate of investment during 1951–7 of £17m. at current prices, or slightly more at 1957 prices. The politicians also accepted that in the past too much emphasis had been placed on long-maturing projects; accordingly, the guide-lines laid down that more public money should go into projects which directly stimulated agricultural and industrial growth, and that in the preparation of other programmes priority should be given to developmental, as opposed to social, needs and to those projects which were likely to yield an immediate economic return.

The actual process of project preparation followed the lines adopted for the Ten-Year Plan. Once again, ministries were asked to submit a list of projects to be considered for inclusion and which they would be able to undertake during the five years of the Plan. The Development Committee/Secretariat had the responsibility of assembling projects submitted into a coherent programme in line with overall priorities. But they were hampered in this work by lack of effective power. The politicians did not have the experience, or collectively the knowledge, and the planners neither the economic expertise nor the influence over either politicians or ministries, to affect the preparation of departmental programmes, or to set precise objectives for individual ministries to follow. The general guidelines which were issued were interpreted differently by the various ministries, where the professional considerations of educationalists or doctors or engineers tended to dominate at the expense of considerations of economic strategy. The Development Committee/Secretariat thus faced the task of sifting projects which had only rarely been subjected to prior economic appraisal, even of a rough and ready kind. The usefulness of the central sifting process was further reduced by the persistence of a crude administrative, instead of economic, approach. Moreover, by deciding not to make preliminary allocations within which individual ministries could prepare their project lists, the Development Committee left the door open to a flood of project proposals far exceeding the upper limit of £100m. set for the total capital budget. Something like this had been expected, and even welcomed, in the belief that it would provide maximum choice and flexibility. But the advantage proved to be illusory: the mere existence of so many project proposals – which ministries claimed to be able to implement within the stipulated five years – made it that much more difficult to exercise control.

In most other African countries such a process of escalation in the capital budget would have mattered little, since the ultimate limit to public investment, whatever was stipulated in development plans, was set by the financial – especially foreign exchange – resources that could be mobilised. But Ghana's case was different: its reserves alone were enough to finance a public sector investment programme almost double the one envisaged in the original Development Committee guidelines. Therefore, since finance did not set an effective absolute limit on spending, sound judgement on the optimal scale of investment, and self-discipline in keeping to it, were particularly important to orderly progress. Though crucial, choosing the optimal scale of investment was not easy. In practice, the choice had to be made by inspired guesswork within a broad political framework, as there was no adequate framework within which investment needs could be considered.

Since the initial guideline range of between £80m. and £100m. was necessarily arbitrary, the fact that ministries felt able to implement more projects than could be accommodated within that range in itself provided ground for its revision. On the other hand, the failure to set ministry limits encouraged ministries to be more ambitious in their programmes, more optimistic about their implementing capacities, and less conscious of costs, than if they had been forced to work within preliminary ministry investment allocations. Because of the acute shortage of skilled people (made worse by the departure of Colonial Officers just before and after independence), and tight Ministry of Finance control over recurrent spending, 'free' access to capital encouraged two biases. First, measures requiring a high capital input were preferred to those needing large recurrent costs or extensive use of skilled personnel; as in the case, for example, when farm mechanisation was given preference over the building up of the extension service. Second, capital projects tended to be more lavish than was perhaps necessary or desirable; this manifested itself, for example, in the design and equipment of hospitals, and other public construction projects such as the university campus at Legon.

The use of existing ministry implementing capacity as a criterion for setting the overall level of investment, and allocating funds between ministries, also hindered the reallocation of funds to quick-maturing investments. Some of the differences in implementing capacity from ministry to ministry were due to their different functions: it was much easier, for example, to prepare (and implement) large infrastructure projects than even small and apparently simple agricultural projects. In general, those ministries whose projects required a relatively large number of skilled personnel were handicapped. Also, officials were more accustomed to dealing with the planning and implementation of capital projects in the areas of public services and social services than in 'directly productive' enterprises, which had traditionally been the almost exclusive province of private initiative. As a result, in the midst of an overabundance of project proposals, few that were put forward fell within the Development Committee's definition of 'productive' and short-maturing investments.

2. The Five-Year Plan (1959–1964)

The new plan was published in March 1959 and was to be implemented over the five years from July 1959 to June 1964; but, for reasons which will be explained in the next section, it was abandoned in the autumn of 1961, and preparations on yet another plan started soon afterwards.

The Five-Year Plan contained an outline programme of public investment costing £250m. Within this 'large coat'[2] plan there was a smaller plan, made up of projects (expected to cost £132m.) which were designated for 'immediate implementation'. The planners had agreed on the lower figure as a realistic target, capable of attainment within the stipulated time-span of the plan. Provisions for recurrent costs and for the financing of capital expenditure were made on that understanding. The politicians, however, did not feel that such a 'modest' investment figure would give the plan the popular appeal they wanted for it. Nkrumah in particular was aware that progress during the coming five years would inevitably leave large sections of the community untouched. He therefore wanted the plan to look impressive, and to make all Ghanaians believe that it could offer something for them. In the end the planners were made to graft on to the original plan an additional £128m. of projects which ministries had submitted for inclusion, but which had originally been left out. On top of that, though separate from the plan, another £100m. was earmarked for an eventual Volta project (see Section 4). But the plan document made it clear that projects additional to the 'small coat' plan were to be implemented only if and when circumstances permitted. The planners themselves did not expect to see many of them started during the plan quinquennium. As for the Volta project, its implementation depended entirely on Ghana's ability to find interested foreign concerns willing to enter into partnership with the government and put up a large part of the finance required.

Although the 'small coat' plan figure of £132m. was much lower than the figure which was arrived at by adding together all the projects which ministries claimed they could have implemented, it was still higher than the figure which conservative opinion – as represented particularly by the Ministry of Finance – considered prudent in the context of revenue estimates. It exceeded by a third the upper figure of the range of £80m. – £100m. which had been laid down in the 1957 planning guidelines. But the compromise figure had the qualified backing of Lewis.

The planned rate of public investment for 1959–64 ('small coat' plan) worked out at £26.4m. a year. In addition, projects costing £15m. were still outstanding from before 1959, and it was hoped to complete these during the term of the plan: this gave a total expected annual investment rate for mid-1959–mid-1964 of almost £30m., double that achieved in the period 1951–8, or 50 percent above the rate in 1954 and 1955, which until then had been the peak years for public investment. The proposed distribution of public investment under the 'small coat' plan is set out in Table 3.1. For comparison, actual investment in the earlier period (1951–8) is also shown.

Agriculture, and manufacturing and mining, the so-called 'productive' sectors, were between them allocated 20 percent of total investment funds. This was double the rate actually recorded in 1951–8.

The planners put much emphasis on agriculture, especially food crops, but did not explain how they had arrived at the chosen figure of £2.1m. (or 8 percent of the total). On the face of it the provision was too small to achieve the planners' aim of developing farming into a 'highly efficient and productive occupation'. But it must be remembered that at this time the role of the public sector was still considered to be limited to providing support services to peasant and large-scale farmers, and it was expected that the greater part of required investment would be made by the farmers themselves. Moreover, agricultural support services relied more on manpower than on capital; and if expected recurrent expenditure is added to investment, the proportion of all public sector expenditure allocated to agriculture rises from 8 percent to over 10 percent. This figure still compared very unfavourably with those in some other African countries; the Ivory

Coast, for example, in its concurrent programme allocated more than a third of all public expenditure to agriculture. In Ghana's case the acute shortage of qualified personnel, combined with a tradition of concentrating available manpower resources on cocoa, were important limiting factors to the government's ability to prepare (and carry out) projects to stimulate the production of food crops.

Table 3.1 Planned distribution of public investment under the Five-Year Plan (annual average)

Sector[1]	Five-Year Plan ('small coat') 1959–1964[2] (£m)	(%)	Past Public Investment (Ten-Year & Consolidation Plans) 1951–1958[3] (£m)	(%)
Agriculture	2.1	(8)	0.9	(6)
Manufacturing and Mining	3.2	(12)	0.6	(4)
Infrastructure and Public Services	8.2	(31)	7.0	(45)
Education	2.9	(11)	2.0	(13)
Health, Social Services and Housing	5.0	(19)	2.0	(13)
General Government	5.0	(19)	2.9	(19)
Total	26.4	(100)	15.5	(100)

Notes:
1. The sectors are the same as in Table 2.1.
2. The Plan was to run, formally, from July 1959 to June 1964; (see also note 3).
3. Ten-Year Plan, January 1951 to June 1957; consolidation 'Plan', July 1957 to December 1958. The consolidation period ended formally in June 1959; but with the publication of the Five-Year Plan in March 1959, its provisions started to be implemented at once.

Sources: **Five-Year Development Plan**
See also Table 2.1 and Statistical Appendix.

The action programme for agriculture (other than cocoa) had the following five priorities: (1) to establish large acreages in rubber and bananas; (2) to study and promote the use of fertilisers; (3) to create the foundations of a cattle industry. (4) to raise the yield of cereals in the North; and (5) to irrigate the Volta plain. At the same time, existing support services – research, extension, and agricultural education – were to be strengthened, the Agricultural Development Corporation (ADC) restructured, and credit stepped up. However, this programme did not amount to a coherent strategy, and did not make clear in what way, and to what extent, the average farmer was supposed to be affected by the measures it listed. It reflected a piecemeal approach, in which projects for tackling a variety of current problems had been hastily assembled. The priorities reflected the preoccupations of the various government bodies which shared responsibility for agricultural policy, and when the plan was launched, little attention had been given to defining their respective roles – for example, the extension service, the co-operatives and the ADC all had their own view of priorities and methods, and continued to operate largely independently of each other. Worse still, all their efforts were directed towards solving specific production problems within the broad objective of 'modernising' farming, rather than towards raising farmer incomes within the broad context of the existing resource endowment of the rural areas.

Similarly, the industrial strategy of the Plan was vague. Its underlying assumption was that the steady improvements in Ghana's infrastructure and public services had already increased the scope for profitable manufacturing industries. The Plan expected that some 600 factories, making over 100 different products, might be started before the end of the plan period. It outlined five areas in which the government would contribute to this process.

The main contribution was to come from continued improvements in infrastructure and public services, for which £41m. was set aside. In addition, general support services – from raw material surveys to business education – were to be stepped up. The government intended also to encourage small-scale African businesses; a study of the best ways of going about this was to be undertaken and an initial £0.5m. was allocated towards implementing its findings. Next, it was planned to continue to encourage investment from overseas by a variety of financial inducements and other forms of help (see Section 4). Finally, the government declared its readiness to step up its involvement, through the IDC, in industrial ventures of a pioneering nature, either on its own or in partnership with private companies. In broad outline the measures were those suggested in 1953 by Lewis; the plan added few details over and above those already published. The one significant difference over the revised Ten-Year Plan was in the financial allocation made to the IDC which, at £2m. a year, was now seven times larger than before.

The Plan did not go into details about the 600 factories that were to be set up. It is therefore not possible to judge how realistic the target was, or what impact on the economy its achievement might have made. However, there was a brief reference to the effect that the factories were to be of 'various sizes'. If this was to mean a preponderance of small establishments (on the existing pattern of Ghanaian manufacturing) then the target of 600 was attainable even without special government help; between 1950 and 1958 some 200 manufacturing establishments employing five or more workers, and as many as 500 employing less than five, had been set up in the private sector. But it is likely that the planners hoped that a substantial number would be large concerns. The Plan itself alluded to the advanced state of negotiations on several partnership arrangements between the IDC and private companies, and to several other industries which the government was determined to promote, all of which were of the large-scale type: some 30 percent of the total IDC budget of £10m. was earmarked for the former, and much of the rest for the latter. Finance for other industrial ventures was expected to come largely from private sources, particularly private overseas sources.

As evidence that the new Plan included more 'productive' projects, which would also yield an economic return in the short run, the planners pointed to the doubling of the investment allocation to agriculture and industry, from 10 percent achieved in 1951–8, to 20 percent planned for 1959–64. On its own, however, this change would not have made a significant difference, for at least two reasons. First, projects within the two so-called 'productive' sectors remained predominantly of the kind that mature only over many years. This was particularly true of agriculture. Of the five priority areas designated (see p.) the last three were essentially long-term. Projects with a potential short-term impact – such as improved extension services, or investment in new storage and processing facilities – were allocated no more than a fifth of total funds for agriculture. Second, projects outside agriculture and industry were not subjected to the requirement of quick-yield. In education, investment in secondary schools was given greater emphasis than before, for developmental reasons. But in general, investments in roads, health, and even education, continued to be made on the basis of ministry views on the best long-term strategy in each of these areas; their impact on the economy was considered only in broad sectoral terms. Thus more feeder-roads, rural clinics, or trade-school courses – to take three random examples – might have made a direct and quick contribution to increasing economic activity in given localities; but they had to wait their turn at the back of the queue because the resources they required were pre-empted by the needs of major schemes aimed at advancing the long-term objectives of the ministries responsible for them. Overall, therefore, in respect of balance between so-called 'productive' and other investments and between short and long maturing projects, the Five-Year Plan was not very different from the Ten-Year Plan. The real difference, in effect, was in the overall investment level.

The new plan was to be financed, as the Ten-Year Plan before it, largely from Ghana's own resources: £115m. (or 80 percent) out of the overall capital requirement of £147m. (£132m. for the 'small coat' plan itself and a further £15m. for projects outstanding from the 'consolidation' period); this compares with two-thirds originally estimated for the Ten-Year Plan, and 97 percent actually raised for projects completed between 1951 and 1958. The balance of £32m. was to be raised by external borrowing; this was £9m. more than in the original estimates for the Ten-Year Plan, but in relative terms 13 percent less than the 33 percent in the earlier plan.

The main difference between the financial provisions of the two plans lay in the way that internal resources were to be mobilised. In the Ten-Year Plan, the domestic requirement was largely expected to be met, and was met, out of current revenue. In the new Five-Year Plan current revenue was expected to finance at best 56 percent and at worst 13 percent of the domestic capital requirement; the rest was to be drawn from the accumulated reserves of the Central Government and the Cocoa Marketing Board. Initially, £50m. was set aside from government reserves and an additional £50m. from CMB reserves. But the extent to which the latter would have to be drawn on was to be determined by the state of the cocoa market; a buoyant market would have allowed the CMB to conserve its reserves and finance its planned contribution of £50m. from current surpluses.

The decision to finance part of the plan from reserves and to maintain momentum in public investment in subsequent plans, had important implications for the future, especially if considered in the context of the likely effect of planned investment on the revenue and foreign exchange position at the end of the plan quinquennium.

Assuming that the most favourable financial assumption made in the plan proved correct, reserves would have financed £50m., and foreign loans another £32m., of public investment. Assuming further that investment thereafter continued at the same rate as planned for 1959–64, and that foreign loans continued to finance the same proportion of total investment, Ghana would have owned just enough free reserves to see it through the next quinquennium, if the cocoa market remained good, but not enough if the cocoa market slumped. Whether, thereafter, the same high rate of public investment was sustainable depended largely on the effect of investment in the 1959–64 Plan on the rate of expansion in both the revenue base and actual revenue, and in exports or the output of import-substitutes.

It is impossible to be definite about the likelihood of the Five-Year Plan's success in these areas. Clearly, public investment was only one – if very important – element of economic policy, and it was always possible that administrative, monetary, fiscal, and other measures would be judiciously deployed to back up public investment. Strict adherence to the capital spending provisions of the 'small coat' plan would have given Ghana steady improvements in infrastructure, public amenities, and social services. The high level of public investment would also have encouraged the growth of the building and construction sector, the service sector, and transport and business enterprises. Increased purchasing power supported by the run-down of reserves and use of foreign credits would have stimulated demand, and in turn the local supply of goods and services already produced in Ghana. But the planners were deceiving themselves in believing that it could have had a significant effect on the production constraints within which Ghanaian agriculture and industry operated. In short, the plan committed Ghana to a long period of dependence on a high level of public capital or recurrent spending, which ultimately could be sustained only by recourse to a progressively larger volume of foreign grants and loans.

3. The 1961 crisis and its effect on policy

From the beginning the government overstepped the spending limits set in the Five-Year Plan. During a three-year period from 1959 to 1961 just over £130m. (or £44m. a year) was spent on public investment; this was £15m. a year more than provided for under the 'small coat' plan (including even the £15m. brought forward from before 1959), and four-fifths of the way towards the spending rate of the propaganda 'large coat' plan. No single factor can explain why this happened. Certainly, there is no record of any deliberate policy decision, either in Cabinet or the Development Committee, to try to complete the 'large coat' investment programme. Ghana, to all appearances, simply drifted into a spending-spree. For this there is no complete explanation either, but a number of contributing factors can be isolated.

First and foremost, there was the imprecise distinction in the Plan document itself between projects intended for the 'small coat' and 'large coat' plans. While the planners had made what they thought to be a clear distinction, the various ministries and public bodies responsible for actual investment decisions seem to have acted according to their own, differing, interpretations. Moreover, while the 'small coat' plan was all that the planners expected to see implemented on the basis of their assessment of the availability of resources, both human and financial, they were ready to give the go-ahead to more projects if their assessment could be shown to be too pessimistic. Ministries could thus expand their programmes simply by cutting down on the preparatory work that the planners had assumed to be necessary. Alternatively, they could supplement their manpower resources by making use of expatriates on short-term technical assistance contracts; such assistance was made available on a scale in excess of anything that was envisaged when the Plan was drawn up.

Ghana's financial resources in the early period of the plan also proved to be more ample than had been expected. It managed to finance 50 percent of capital spending out of recurrent budget surpluses, which was at the optimistic end of the expected range of 13–56 percent; the case for restricting capital spending to the level of the 'small coat' plan was thereby considerably weakened. Moreover, even with a less strong revenue position, it would have been difficult to contain capital spending once the rate at which projects were put forward for financing exceeded the rate envisaged in the 'small coat' plan. The planners had, for one thing, failed to provide a proper time-table for phasing investment over the quinquennium. Such phasing had been previously achieved through the Capital Estimates in the Budget, which had to be submitted for annual legislative approval; this had kept proposed annual investment to a level consistent with annual revenue or available loan finance. But since up to £100m. of resources had already been allocated to the Five-Year Plan from reserves, the link between need and availability in any one year had disappeared and the Estimates no longer provided an automatic check.

Another factor which inflated capital spending was the imprecise nature of many of the original project proposals. In some cases capital needs were badly underestimated. In others, the initial vagueness in the proposals permitted considerable latitude – often encouraged by ministers or other interested politicians (or even contractors) – for extending the scope of projects, or improving specifications. Straightforward inflationary effects must also be taken into account: prices rose quickly in 1960 and 1961; the introduction of minimum wage legislation in July 1960 alone added between 5 percent and 10 percent to the cost of the 'small coat' plan.

These factors contributed to the build-up in pressure for more and quicker capital spending, and were difficult to resist. But the most important pressure was Nkrumah's political determination to push ahead with development. It is clear that his drive and enthusiasm were crucial. And yet Nkrumah's personal determination would have been of less consequence if it had not been for the large number of ambitious, forceful, and capable Ghanaians and expatriates who had the ability to organise, arrange, and implement the programmes he inspired. The rate of spending on capital projects achieved in 1959–61 and the technical standards of completed projects testify to their considerable skill and organising capacity. At the same time, it is doubtful whether a programme of this size would have been launched, and pursued with such determination, had those responsible for it been more experienced and more versed in the complexities of economic development. This was Ghana's paradox, and indeed tragedy: its administration and its politicians had the capacity to do a great deal that was ambitious, but not the capacity to judge what it was best to do.

The great upsurge of capital investment between 1959 and 1961 had several adverse consequences: it trapped the government into maintaining, for political reasons, a high level of public investment during a period when Ghana could no longer afford it; it increased recurrent expenditure (needed to maintain and make use of completed projects) to a level where this absorbed the bulk of tax revenue; it overstrained the available supply of skilled personnel, thereby reducing the efficiency with which new and existing public services were run; it competed with the private sector for scarce resources, particularly construction capacity and a wide range of managerial, technical, and clerical skills; it accustomed a still larger number of people to imported manufactured goods and further increased Ghana's dependence on imports; it made Ghana dependent on foreign grants and loans much sooner than the planners had envisaged; and, finally, it prompted the government to draw the wrong policy conclusions.

The most immediate consequence which had to be faced at the end of 1961 was the rapidly deteriorating foreign exchange position. During 1959–61 GDP had increased at an average annual rate of 9.1 percent in real terms. This rate was sustained largely by capital and recurrent public spending, which had increased from £54m. in 1958 to £116m. in 1961; as a result, in 1959–61 budget deficits of £8m., £28m. and £29m. were recorded. Because of the high import content in investment and the high propensity to import out of additional income generated by public spending, the import bill rose from £95m. in 1958 to £163m. in 1961. At the same time exports rose by much less, from £110m. in 1958 to £122m. in 1961. The balance of payments on current account thus turned from a surplus of £11m. in 1958, to a deficit of the same amount in 1959; and by 1961 the deficit had gone up to £52m. Government reserves fell sharply, and Ghana's *foreign* reserves even more (despite a £25m. inflow of medium-term capital towards the public sector investment budget) from £178m. at the end of 1958, to £149m. at the end of 1960, and £73m. at the end of 1961. Had this rate of depletion continued unchecked, Ghana's foreign reserves would have vanished during 1962–3.

In spite of this, the government saw no reason for curbing public spending. Instead, it decided to initiate massive import-substitution programmes, in both agriculture and industry, and to curb imports by imposing in early 1961 additional duties and import levies; when imports continued to rise rigid controls were introduced both on imports and on a wide range of exchange transactions. In addition, the government mobilised the foreign exchange reserves still held by institutions, including commercial banks, public corporations and the Cocoa Marketing Board.

Import-substitution had long been implicit in Nkrumah's goal of 'restructuring'. But it was not until 1961 that it came to be described specifically in these terms. The change from 'productive investments' to 'import substitution' (and 'export promotion') is significant, because it reflects the fact that it took a balance of payments crisis to convince Nkrumah that continuing with the type of capital investment programme provided for in the Five-Year Plan could not bring the dramatic improvements in agriculture and industry that he wanted. The crisis contributed also to Nkrumah's loss of faith in the ability of Ghanaian private entrepreneurs (and foreign investors) to take advantage of the opportunities which he believed to have been created for them by public investment. In fact, Ghanaian entrepreneurs had responded, at least to the demand created by public spending: manufacturing, for instance, had by 1961 increased its share in GDP to nearly 10 percent, from a mere 4 percent in 1950–53. However, these figures were not available at the time, while it was obvious, on the other hand, that few large-scale manufacturing establishments had come into being since Nkrumah had come to office. He now became interested in the proposal, long ago put forward by the most radical members of the CPP, that Ghana should by-pass the private sector and instead expand the scope of state-run industrial and agricultural undertakings, thereby promoting directly the objectives of import-substitution and export diversification. In August 1961 Nkrumah visited the Soviet Union and other East European countries; his decision to expand state-enterprise, while preceding this good-will tour, was nevertheless much reinforced by it.

State enterprise, while fraught with dangers, was not necessarily inappropriate to Ghana's needs; but the decision to make it a corner-stone of policy stemmed from the wrong premise. A determined drive to expand import-substitutes, particularly if the emphasis was to be placed at least as much on agriculture as on industry, was a sound enough policy; but it could not be expected to show any significant results in the short run. Moreover, industrial manufacturing would inevitably add to, rather than reduce, the foreign exchange bill in the initial phase. It offered, therefore, no effective solution for many years to come to the basic foreign exchange problem. Import and exchange controls could certainly provide some breathing space, if efficiently applied – which they were not. But in any case, given the 1961 current account deficit of £52m., and with consumer imports (other than food) accounting for less than a third of all imports, it was not enough to curb consumer imports alone if enough foreign exchange was to be saved to pay for imports of components, materials, and fuels needed for expanding domestic production, and for the direct foreign exchange costs of capital projects. The successful implementation of the import-substitution programme itself required curbs also on less essential, or long-maturing, capital projects, particularly those with major recurrent cost implications.

Nkrumah believed, however, that foreign borrowing offered a simple way of avoiding cut-backs in the total volume of investment already planned. In mid-1961 he was able to announce that Ghana could count on external 'financial resources of the order of £250m. for the purpose of development expenditure – a sum that is sufficient to cover the maximum that we can profitably spend (overseas) for many years to come'.[3] Even so, this decision to embark on major new programmes, while maintaining the rate of spending on old programmes, was ill-considered. Gbedemah, Nkrumah's most important political ally and probably his ablest minister, recognised this, but his firm opposition merely drove him out of office. Nkrumah persisted, and his persistence was to be the direct cause of Ghana's rapid plunge into debt, and into a serious debt problem.

4. The forging of new links with suppliers of external resources

In the period 1957–61 Ghana established important new links with the Soviet Union and other communist countries, discovered how easy it was to raise substantial credits from exporters of capital goods, and negotiated finance for the Volta Project; but it failed otherwise to interest overseas investors. In 1957 foreign loans were only contemplated; by the end of 1961 Ghana had used £25m., and signed contracts totalling in all £190m. (see Table 4.3). In 1957 foreign finance was needed, but not urgently; by the end of 1961 it had become indispensable to Nkrumah's entire economic programme, and almost certainly also to his political survival. In 1957 Ghana looked forward to a period of fruitful co-operation with Western governments; by the end of 1961, when its need for such co-operation had become much greater, its alienation from both Britain and the United States had begun. In 1957, Ghana also looked forward to an increasing flow of private investment capital; in 1961 it had to introduce controls to prevent the flight of capital.

i) Official aid from the West

At independence, Ghana approached the United Nations and a large number of countries in search of assistance, particularly technical assistance. By the end of 1957, agreements were signed with the UN, Britain and the US, followed in 1958 by agreements with West Germany, the Scandinavian countries, and the Netherlands, and later with Yugoslavia and Taiwan. The first country to give help was Israel, although no formal assistance agreement was signed. The agreements with the UN, Britain and the US were of very considerable importance; but the others were, in the main, little more than gestures of support on Ghana's entry into the international community as an independent state.

Ghana's post-independence Five-Year Plan, it will be recalled, was based on the expectation of a minimum of £32m. in external loans towards the capital budget. However, the government made only a half-hearted effort to raise this finance; partly because its own substantial resources provided a breathing space, and partly because it had little doubt that its credit standing (given its minute foreign debt and large reserves) would enable it, in time, to raise loans without difficulty. But sources of finance to which Ghana could turn were, perhaps contrary to its expectations, limited. In the first place, Ghana had no real experience of raising loans in international capital markets. Second, official sources were restricted: in practice, Ghana could look only to the British and American governments and to the World Bank, and even then not with complete certainty; of the other major donors, France concentrated on its own dependencies and ex-dependencies, while West Germany, whose programme was growing rapidly and which had as yet no settled geographic pattern, considered that Africa was in need more of technical assistance than of financial aid.

Pre-independence British capital aid to Ghana had effectively come to an end in 1954 (see Chapter 2); at independence Ghana received only a grant of £0.4m., equivalent to the unspent part of its post-war CD&W allocation. In September 1958, at the Montreal Commonwealth Finance Ministers' Conference, Britain reversed its formal policy of not continuing regular financial aid to ex-colonies reaching independence. Ghana, however, did not benefit immediately, while India and Pakistan, both of which then faced balance of payments difficulties, obtained very large loans. Ghana appears to have been disqualified by its relative wealth, and even more by its healthy foreign exchange reserve position; the latter had indeed effectively disqualified from aid both India and Pakistan when they became independent.

The United States did not wish, so long as African countries remained European dependencies, to involve itself in more than a very limited way. It considered, also, that even after independence, the main responsibility for aid should remain with the relevant ex-metropolitan power. Its own involvement was confined to countries without European colonial ties, such as Ethiopia and Liberia; elsewhere it intervened with substantial financial assistance only when strategic interests, as in Libya and Morocco, or special political circumstances, as in Tunisia and the former Belgian Congo, dictated. In other parts of Africa the United States confined itself to offering technical assistance – and where appropriate food aid; tokens of support to show that it wished to be identified with 'African aspirations for political and economic development'.[4] However, the US aid programme has always defined technical assistance widely, so that it could include, on occasion, a large capital component. An offer of US technical assistance could, therefore, be much like an offer of capital aid from other donors, with the additional advantage of an integral technical support component; and Ghana did in fact secure some US capital aid by this route for agricultural extension, business training, and health.

The World Bank, the remaining important Western source of finance, was at the time of Ghana's independence engaged almost entirely in the financing of sound infrastructure projects. Its main concern, besides ensuring the financial and technical viability of projects, was with the credit-worthiness of countries in which project-finance was contemplated. The Bank's criteria of credit-worthiness, among which the ratio of overseas debt to export earnings was prominent, presented no problems to Ghana. It had decided to become a member of the Bank soon after independence, and preliminary discussions on possible projects were held immediately its membership had been approved. However, since the process of negotiating Bank loans was particularly exacting and complex, it was inevitable that no firm proposals could emerge for some time. Later the Bank became involved in the Volta Project.

ii) The Volta River Project

The Volta Project remained an exception in Ghana's dealings with suppliers of external resources. Not only did the government make strenuous efforts over a long period to secure finance and the participation of leading expatriate companies, but it was also ready to accept the advice, and conditions imposed by the providers of finance. The project assumed such an overwhelming political, psychological, and developmental importance for Nkrumah that for long periods all other negotiations on external finance were subordinated to its needs.

The Volta River Project had first been mooted in the 1920s. It was revived again in the 1940s by the British government's anxiety to secure new supplies of aluminium from outside the Dollar Area. A report on the economic potential of an aluminium smelter, using water for electric power from the Volta River, was published at the time of the 1951 Ghana elections. It was favourable. Nkrumah was at once determined that the project should be given the go-ahead, and negotiations were started with the British government and several British aluminium companies. The first practical results emerged in the 1952 agreement to set up a Volta River Project Preparatory Commission (VRPPC), which was to prepare a detailed plan; the costs of this work were to be shared equally between the British and Ghanaian governments. In 1956 VRPPC produced plans for an integrated aluminium industry, using the hydro-electric power from a proposed dam across the Volta at Ajena, and bauxite from unexploited deposits nearby. Reference was also made to the possibility of using surplus water for an irrigation scheme in the Accra plain, water transport on the lake formed by the dam, and the development of a lake fishing industry. The total cost of the dam, the hydro-electric power station, the aluminium smelter, and ancilliary installations was put at £230m. By 1956, however, all but one of the aluminium companies originally interested had dropped out; the British government, too, had second thoughts, following the rapid expansion in world aluminium output and the easing of the post-war dollar shortage. The scheme was shelved, to be revived again by Nkrumah at independence.

Nkrumah sought the support of the American government through a personal appeal to President Eisenhower. The scheme attracted the interest of the head of the Kaiser Corporation, on whose authority a scaled-down version of the VRPPC scheme was worked out. The new scheme was to include a Volta dam and hydro-electric station at Akosombo, and an aluminium smelter at Tema, based on Akosombo electric power and imported alumina. Kaiser's contribution was to consist of the building, financing, and operating of the £44m. smelter. The main change from the VRPPC scheme was in the proposed use of imported alumina, which required only an aluminium smelter, rather than an integrated alumina-aluminium complex. In the Kaiser scheme no mention was made of the earlier irrigation plans for the Accra plain; and the other elements, making up the original package – lake fishing and transport development – were kept separate from the main scheme, and their detailed consideration was postponed. Kaiser insisted, also, on substantial concessions in the form of tax relief and minimal charges for the electricity used by the smelter. The Kaiser scheme received the backing of the US government, and with this assurance Ghana approached the World Bank for financial help. Agreement was reached in 1961 on a Bank loan of £17m., within an overall package to which the American and British governments were also to contribute. The overall cost and sources of finance for the scheme are set out on the opposite page.

The World Bank had estimated that the investment in the dam and hydro-electric scheme would give a return on capital of 8–8.5 percent over its entire life of at least forty years. This rate of return was only a little better than the minimum the Bank required to give financial support to a project. The net contribution to GDP of the

Table 3.2 The Volta River Project

1. Akosombo dam and power station	£m.	
World Bank	16.8	(at 5¾ percent over 25 years)
US (AID)	9.6	(at 3½ percent over 25 years)
US (Ex-Im Bank)	3.6	(at 5¾ percent over 25 years)
Britain	5.0	(at 6 percent over 25 years)
Total external loan finance	35.0	
Ghana government	35.0	(Equity)
Total cost	70.0	
2. Tema aluminium smelter (VALCO)		
Kaiser Corporation)	44.0	(Equity 90 percent)
Reynolds Corporation)		(Equity 10 percent)
3. Ancillary investment at Tema		
Ghana government	7.2	
Total investment	121.2	

Source: The Volta River Project, Government Printer, Accra, 1961.

entire project, including the smelter when fully operational, was put at only £7–£8m. a year; this represented 1½ percent of Ghana's actual GDP in 1961 (and about 1¼ percent of its achieved real GDP in 1969, the year in which the smelter reached normal output). Aside from the temporary employment opportunities created during the construction phase, the contribution of the VRP to employment was expected to be modest – some 200 at Akosombo and at most 1,500 in the smelter itself and at the port of Tema. However, the net foreign exchange earnings from the smelter, when fully operational, were expected to amount to between £16m. and £19m. a year; this would have made the smelter the second largest earner of foreign exchange, with an earning capacity equal to one-fifth of annual cocoa exports.

The Volta River Project, as originally conceived by the VRPPC, was to have been a more expensive and also much more ambitious venture. The dam, hydro-electric, and integrated aluminium industry complex were seen as the hub from which would spread out a variety of connected activities – bauxite mining, irrigated agriculture, lake fishing and transport, and industry. For its most ardent supporters, this project, in its original form, had become both vehicle and symbol of a total transformation of the Ghanaian economy. For these supporters, particularly the radical members of the CPP, the decision to negotiate on the basis of the scaled-down Kaiser version amounted to a sell-out. Their anger was compounded by the fear that Ghana's newly-won political independence would be nullified by the economic dominance – particularly through control over the Volta Project – of foreign business interests; it was inconceivable to them that Nkrumah could contemplate entrusting a venture, which above all offered Ghana a chance of freeing itself from a subservient 'colonial' economic role, to those very interests which had helped to confine Ghana to that role. In response to their protests, and partly as a lever in the Kaiser negotiations, Nkrumah initiated parallel negotiations with the Russians; and indeed feasibility studies by Russian experts for an alternative to the Akosombo dam were started. Work continued even after Nkrumah's commitment to the Kaiser proposals, but was eventually suspended by the Russians once Nkrumah had lost all interest in this alternative.

Opposition to the Volta Project was not confined to the left wing of the CPP. The Ministry of Finance, most notably, had greeted the VRPPC report with undisguised displeasure, since at the time it was particularly concerned to reduce public spending on long-maturing projects (see Chapter 2). Although the scaled-down Kaiser version was less objectionable, the Ministry remained anxious – in spite of the enthusiastic support of the Minister himself – to avoid committing the vast resources that were required on this single, long-maturing project. Moreover, although under the financing agreement almost half of the Ghanaian contribution was to be met from long-term overseas loans, the Ministry considered that other projects were more urgent and that loan finance should first be secured for those. In view of the earlier difficulties Ghana had experienced in trying – admittedly not very hard – to raise long-term loans in the West, it is possible that those donors who were interested in financing Volta would have lost all interest in Ghana if that project had been abandoned. But allowing even for that eventuality the Ministry had a strong case. In the first place, while the World Bank considered the Volta Project viable, it had not been asked to make an assessment of its relative priority in relation to alternative uses of funds. In the second place, the Bank's estimate of the overall impact on the economy was much more modest than the project's Ghanaian backers claimed. Ghana was, therefore, clearly taking a considerable risk in committing as much as £77m. in the venture, a sum equivalent to more than half of the total capital budget for all other public sector projects which the planners expected to be completed in 1959–64. Nkrumah's own attitude to the project suggested that he was interested, above all, in the prestige and the drawing power for private capital – particularly overseas capital – that Volta signified. It was his persistence, backed up by Gbedemah until his resignation in 1961, which carried the day.

iii) Private foreign investment

The Five-Year Plan industrial proposals were based on a substantial, though unquantified, contribution in the form of direct investment from abroad. The Plan repeated the government's favourable attitude to such investment and its determination to accord it fair treatment and security, provided certain rules were observed. These included recognition of trade unions, training of Africans for high-level posts, and the development of local sources of raw material wherever this was feasible (a rule which was waived in the case of the Kaiser aluminium smelter). The government also designated a number of industries which were reserved for the public sector (broadly all public utilities); and several others where government participation was mandatory (broadly, those concerned with the manufacture of drugs and alcoholic beverages). All other industries, including most manufacturing industries, were declared open to private enterprise, foreign as well as local. It was hoped that, by making explicit the government's thinking, and by laying down firm guidelines in advance, misunderstandings which might deter potential investors could be avoided, and the adverse publicity generated by opponents of private investment could be offset. As a positive encouragement to overseas investment the government had, even before the publication of the Plan, increased the value of the incentives that were available, including tax and import duty concessions. These were to supplement the help, both financial and other, offered through the Industrial Development Corporation.

Until the end of 1961 the government's treatment of expatriate enterprises was liberal. There was no discrimination of any kind, no expropriation, or threat of it, and no control over capital or profit remittance. When a number of gold mines threatened to go out of operation following the introduction of a statutory minimum wage in 1960, the government bought them out; but at a fair price, on the companies' own admission.

All the same, for a variety of reasons, partly associated with the depressed state of the economy and the uncertainty surrounding independence, the flow of *new* private investment had been reduced to a trickle during 1957–9; overall there was a net outward flow of capital amounting to £8m. By the end of 1959 the situation had stabilised; led by the larger expatriate companies, foreign investment picked up again and there was a modest £2m. net inflow in 1960. The Five-Year Plan itself attracted considerable interest from overseas. During its first year (1959–60) ten survey teams from seven countries came to Ghana to make on-the-spot appraisals of opportunities. They submitted some eighty projects for consideration by the IDC; but nothing came of them. Despite buoyant business conditions and Ghana's exemplary record towards foreign business, these potential newcomers judged that underlying conditions were not yet favourable enough for investment in new ventures. One obstacle to investment in import-substitute industries, for instance, was the ease with which imports could be brought into what was then still a very limited market; this had already proved a severe handicap for at least three of the eight factories which had been set up before 1959 under the auspices of the IDC. Thus, apart from the special case of the Kaiser aluminium smelter, Ghana had to be satisfied with only a few new private, or private state, manufacturing ventures initiated by already established expatriate concerns, most notably the United Africa Company. This experience reinforced Nkrumah's earlier disappointment that private investment had contributed so little to his industrial plans; by 1961 he saw no real alternative to a change in the role of the public sector, from one of general support of private enterprise to one of catalyst of industrial development through direct state participation on a large scale. This change was made possible by the willingness of Western companies – and later of Eastern governments – to supply on credit the factories, equipment, know-how and, sometimes, technical and managerial expertise, which were beyond Ghana's own capacity to organise and finance.

iv) East European loans

Ghana's formal efforts to raise aid were until 1960 confined entirely to Western sources. But, as long ago as 1951, when Nkrumah had stated that he would be 'appealing to the democracies of Britain and the United States for assistance in the first place', he had also added that if this should not be forthcoming, he 'would be forced to turn elsewhere'.[5] At the time, by 'elsewhere', he could only have meant the Soviet Union. Later, at independence, Nkrumah was urged by a number of leading CCP radicals to follow up this earlier hint. When by 1960 Ghana had not secured a single official loan from the West, an approach to the East had become more necessary; by then it also fitted neatly into Nkrumah's aggressive new policy of non-alignment.

In the meantime, at the Cairo conference of Afro-Asian countries in 1958, the Soviet Union had announced its intention to offer aid in 'unlimited quantities and without strings'[6] to any developing country requesting it. The first aid agreement with Russia, signed in 1960, followed from that offer, although some groundwork had been done even before 1958 – unknown to Nkrumah – by Soviet sympathisers in the CPP. The 1960 agreement was for loans and technical assistance worth – nominally – £21.5m.; later in the year the figure was revised to £30m. Agreements with a number of other East European countries followed Nkrumah's 1961 good-will tour. Up to the end of 1961, some £3m. was disbursed; but the main flow was not to come until the mid-1960s.

Ghana was one of four countries in Black Africa to receive promises of substantial Russian aid – the others being Ethiopia, Guinea and Mali. The nominal value of aid promised (at different dates for the various countries) was about £30m. in each case; in addition, Sudan and Somalia were each promised about £10m. and a number of other countries token sums or technical assistance. Ghana's slice of Russian aid was not as big as that going to India, Indonesia, Afghanistan, UAR, and Algeria – each of these received offers valued at between four and ten times that for Ghana – but in terms of aid *per capita* Ghana was, nevertheless, Russia's fourth biggest client (after Algeria, Afghanistan, and Guinea) outside the communist world.

There is little information on the motives which lay behind the distribution of Russian aid offers. The most obvious factor seems to have been the attitude of the various recipients themselves. Generally speaking, all those countries which approached Russia, especially after the Cairo offer, got something; and the full amount disbursed was determined largely by the length of time over which an aid relationship continued. It may be noted that at the time when the Black African countries approached Russia for aid, all of them (except Ethiopia) were either openly quarrelling with their respective metropolitan powers or, particularly in Ghana's case, had found it difficult to attract aid from the West.

Apart from the obvious attraction of Russia as an additional source of aid, there was also its declared attitude towards 'aid-strings'. This was particularly welcomed by those countries, such as Ghana, which were trying to assert themselves vigorously as independent, non-aligned new nations. Russia's promise not to impose political strings and to abide by the wishes of recipients when it came to determining aid use appears to have been prompted by the overall wish to gain good-will and – a related point – to demonstrate the 'superiority' of its aid over that offered by the Americans and other Western donors. Initially, the practical effect of Russia's 'aid without strings' policy was that it did not look very closely at Ghana's demands before agreeing to help with projects. After only a short period, however, Russia was urging Ghana – for its own commercial reasons – to accept particular projects or equipment; the sale of Ilyushin aircraft is a case in point. At the same time, Ghana found that Russian personnel were often as critical as any from the West, and they recommended, for technical or economic reasons, that some of the schemes put up by Ghana should be rejected or substantially modified. It was, for example, Russia's reluctance on grounds of economic viability to support Ghana's plans in the textile field which made the latter accept an ill-fated alternative offer from French machinery suppliers.[7]

Other Eastern-bloc countries followed Russia's lead, if sometimes only reluctantly. Poland, in particular, resented Russian pressure on its Comecon partners to follow its aid lead; it considered that its own contribution was merely relieving Russia of some of the costs of a Russian programme designed largely to promote Russian interests. Nevertheless, given that some contribution from them was required, these countries saw in 'aid' an opportunity for broadening their trade.

The sale to Ghana of equipment which had no ready market in the West – even though relatively generous credit terms had to be offered to Ghana – provided them with an additional source of badly needed hard currency. (This was of particular importance, too, for Yugoslavia.) However, the combined effect of their reluctance to give aid and their appreciation of a commercial opportunity offering some compensation for having to follow Russia's lead, was to make East European projects in many ways indistinguishable from those financed by private suppliers' credits (see Chapter 4).

v) Supplier credits

Ghana's considerable financial assets and ambitious programme of public investment following independence attracted a large number of foreign contractors, manufacturers of plant and equipment, agents and promoters. Their main interest was to sell, and their trump card an offer of credit. Ghana's first credit contract, £0.9m. for the supply of buses, was signed with the Leyland Company of Manchester in December 1959; the credit was to be repaid over five years and carried a rate of interest of 5½ percent. Up to the end of 1961, a total of at least fourteen contracts were signed, valued at more than £17m. (see Table 4.3), all but three with British companies. Ten of the contracts (accounting for half the value of credits offered) were for periods of between three and five years, the others for periods of seven and eight years. The typical interest rate was 6 per cent, with a weighted average of a fraction over that.

The credits signed in 1959 and 1960 made no more than a negligible contribution to Ghana's external capital needs during the Plan quinquennium, since nearly all were scheduled for full repayment by 1964. Moreover, prices on credit sales were inflated, and the interest rates charged were somewhat higher than the current yield on Ghana's external assets; so in fact, Ghana had to pay a small premium for the privilege of substituting temporary credit for an immediate encashment of sterling assets. On the other hand, buying on credit did make it easier to arrange for the sale of financial assets at the most favourable moment. Overall, the advantages and disadvantages were fairly evenly balanced. By 1961, with Ghana's external assets already dwindling as a result of the need to finance rising imports, there was no longer the same scope for choosing between the alternatives of asset disposal and credit buying; to maintain momentum in public investment Ghana had to secure external credits for as high a proportion of capital imports as it could arrange. Even though their average maturity was relatively short, credits did at least provide bridging finance. But whether they made sense in the longer run depended, first, on the impact of Ghana's entire investment programme on its net foreign exchange earnings, and second, on the net foreign exchange contribution of the projects financed with external credit.

In an earlier comment on the Five-Year Plan (see Section 2) it was shown that there was room for doubt as to whether public investment in the 'small coat' plan was capable of increasing revenue and net foreign exchange earnings by an amount sufficient to allow Ghana to continue financing public investment after 1964 without having to borrow more and more from abroad. *A fortiori*, recourse to loans with an average maturity of five years, for financing investments over and above the level of the 'small coat' plan, could only cast still greater doubt. As to the plant and equipment supplied under credit agreements signed up to the end of 1961, its use can be divided in roughly equal proportions between 'productive' and 'prestige' projects. Among the former were tractors, buses, outboard motors, fishing vessels, navigation and telecommunications equipment, and, with some reservations, crop-spraying and short-range passenger aircraft. However, the VC-10 aircraft and eight merchant ships (costing in all £14m., with credit for £9m.) were 'luxuries' that Ghana could have done without. Their purchase was not foreseen in the Five-Year Plan, nor indeed was the purchase of some of the other items. Rather, the government appears to have been talked into making them by determined salesmanship; although in many cases the salesmen were met at least half-way by Nkrumah or other government ministers. While foreign companies played on the ambitions of individuals or groups to promote particular ventures, individual ministers, or representatives of departments, public bodies or local authorities used offers of credit to advance their own favourite projects, thus avoiding the need to compete for a share of domestic funds or administrative resources. In the end, foreign credits not only helped to finance projects included in the Plan, but generated their own momentum for increased public spending outside the framework of the Plan. In 1961, following Nkrumah's decision to embark on a major programme of state industries, and the negotiation of credits with East European countries for the supply and installation of entire plants or factories, a new field opened up for enterprising Western companies. And even though by the end of 1961 Ghana's credit-worthiness was no longer assured, export credit insurance available from their own governments allowed them to exploit the new opportunity to the full, and allowed the Ghana government to raise, but on harsh terms, the external resources which it could not raise through long-term aid.

Notes

1. Development Committee Circular.
2. The designations 'large coat' and 'small coat' (see below) stem from a remark in the legislature that Ghana should cut its coat to suit its cloth.
3. National Assembly Debates, 1961, Vol.IV, Col.16.
4. *Mutual Security Program,* 1958–9 (Summary presentation to Congress), p.75.
5. Speech quoted in *Ghana* (Nkrumah's autobiography), Nelson, 1959, p.136.
6. Quoted in *Mutual Security Program, 1958/9.* loc.cit.
7. See Chapter 4, Section 4(iii).

Chapter 4 The Plunge into Insolvency (1962-1965)

1. Government control over the economy

In the last few months of 1961 and the first few months of 1962, a series of administrative, monetary and fiscal measures were introduced which transformed the 'open', largely market-oriented, economy of Ghana into a 'closed', tightly controlled one. Exchange control for capital transactions was extended to Sterling Area countries. Restrictions on the external operations of the banks were imposed, particularly by the requirement that a proportion of their assets should be kept in newly created Ghana government securities. Ghana completed the change-over from the colonial Currency Board system to a fully fledged Central Bank system (with full local control over the issuing of money) thus severing the remaining formal links between foreign reserves and the domestic money supply. The Bank of Ghana took over Sterling securities held by public corporations and private institutions, in exchange for Ghana government securities. Exchange control was imposed on current transactions, particularly through the import licensing system. Monopoly rights were granted to the Ghana Trading Corporation to import a wide range of staple commodities. Barter and other trade agreements with a number of East European countries were concluded. The cocoa market was moved from London to Accra and the government export monopoly was extended to diamonds and a number of lesser export products.

The first six of the measures were almost certainly inevitable sooner or later; they would no doubt have been introduced earlier had it not been for Ghana's healthy reserve position at independence. Moreover, their earlier, gradual, and carefully prepared introduction would almost certainly have been to Ghana's advantage. However the need for, or the potential advantage to be gained from, the other measures were less obvious. In all, the sudden extension of government control over large areas of economic activity implied by these measures placed a new and massive burden on the bureaucracy which it was not yet capable of carrying. The measures, therefore, created initial uncertainty through their inept and often arbitrary administration; later, any advantage that Ghana derived from them in some areas -- such as the conservation of foreign exchange – was more than offset by the chaos and disruption they caused in others, particularly by increasing the opportunities for corruption and stifling the weaker among African enterprises.

The primary consideration, common to all the measures, was to defend Ghana's balance of payments position, both by restrictions and by more positive moves to tap new sources of foreign exchange. A secondary consideration was to secure for government use all the revenue and capital that could be squeezed out of the existing system. But the urgency of both was, in the end, determined by the government's anxiety to push on with its massive investment programme. The choice and form of several of the measures were prompted in part also by Nkrumah's increasing preoccupation with accelerating the 'decolonisation' of Ghana's economy and protecting it from continued – as he saw it – foreign exploitation. The extension of monopoly privileges to Ghanaian state corporations, the removal of the cocoa market from London, the negotiation of trade agreements with East European countries all come under this heading. The influence of the decolonisation aim manifested itself most clearly in the new policy guidelines adopted by the CCP Congress in July 1962. These called for the building of 'a socialist state which accepts full responsibility for promoting the well-being of the masses'; they stressed, too, that socialism would 'remain a slogan until industrialisation (was) achieved', and that socialism required a different kind of economic structure 'from the type that was evolved by the colonial administration'.[1] Although couched in often nebulous terms borrowed from communist jargon, the guidelines were a neat rationalisation of the government's policies of economic restructuring through massive public investment, state enterprise and state direction.

The guidelines called for comprehensive planning of a kind which had not as yet been tried in Ghana. The actual decision to scrap the Five-Year Plan, made in late 1961, and to start work on a new plan using a more sophisticated planning framework and techniques, was taken after Nkrumah's tour of Russia. According to E. N. Omaboe, then Chief Government Statistician, Nkrumah was much impressed by Russia's current (seven-year) plan, and the planning methods used; on his return to Ghana he became dissatisfied with the Five-Year Plan, which he dismissed as a 'collection of puny projects'. While Ghana's mixed enterprise economy and lack of an adequate statistical base made the full Russian planning model unsuitable, the planners did try to provide a plan which was different from the colonial public sector 'shopping list' approach and much closer to the Russian model. Out of these efforts Ghana's Seven-Year Plan emerged, incorporating for the first time quantitative targets for GDP and its main components, and based on a model – albeit a crude one – of the economy.

The introduction of the measures listed earlier had extended – in theory at least – the government's powers of direction and control over the private sector. It was hoped that the new planning approach, by extending the scope of planning to the private sector, would take the process of state control and direction an important stage further. However, in Ghana's circumstances, the main advantage of comprehensive planning was that it improved the understanding of forces operating in the economy, and of the respective roles required of the public and private sectors if certain objectives were to be met. In practical terms, therefore, comprehensive national planning was most valuable in providing guidance for the best deployment of resources within the public sector. Over and above that, through the advance publication of government investment intentions and indicative targets for the private sector, planning could help to guide private decisions. But indicative targets on their own could not force the private sector to act in the manner the government desired; targets had to be backed up by monetary, fiscal, administrative, and other measures. Having started with the idea that the new planning approach would help to enhance the government's influence over the private sector, the planners were forced to conclude that they had inadequate instruments at hand; and, in the end, this fact provided an additional rationale for enlarging the public sector itself.

2. The formulation of the Seven-Year Plan (1964–70)

The Seven-Year Plan was intended to provide a detailed strategy for the implementation of the 'first phase' of Ghana's policy of developing import-substitutes and new exports through state-run industry and agriculture, first announced by Nkrumah in 1961, and confirmed at the CPP congress a year later. The 'first phase' was to cover the period from October 1963 to September 1970. The Plan was not approved, however, until March 1964; as a result of the delay and the adjustment in the dates of the financial year, the first phase was thus redated January 1964–December 1970. The projections, quantitative targets, and assumptions contained in the Plan were based on statistics which were already dated when it was published; figures beyond 1961 (or occasionally 1962) were not available to the planners, and since a great deal had happened in 1962 and 1963, the plan was out of gear from the beginning, although formally it remained in effect until Nkrumah's fall from power in February 1966. Despite its short life, the Plan is nevertheless of considerable interest because it sets out, on the one hand, the objectives in pursuit of which Ghana acquired its massive foreign debt and, on the other, the extent to which the planners expected to rely on external capital, public and private.

GDP over the plan period was expected to grow at an average annual rate of 5.5 percent, compared with 6.4 percent achieved over 1958–61 (the base from which the planners worked), and 4.1 percent in the two pre-Plan years 1962–3 (a figure which was, however, not then available). The cautious expectation, in fact justified by the 1962–3 figures, was based largely on a pessimistic view of the state of the cocoa market, which also proved correct. The planners expected a rate of growth in what they called 'basic production' of 7.5 percent a year (or 8 percent excluding cocoa); basic production included cash crops, mining, construction, public utilities and modern (i.e. non-traditional) manufacturing. This compared with 6 percent (or 5.5 percent excluding cocoa) achieved in 1955–62, which was the planning base period for these sectors.

The planners expected that the growth rates stipulated in basic production and GDP would be achieved with a total volume of investment of £1,015m. over the seven years. Of this a notional £100m. was to be direct labour contributions in the agricultural sector, involving no cash transactions (e.g. farmers clearing land or otherwise improving farms). The rest, £915m. or £130m. a year, represented the required cash outlay on investment. Of this, £475m. (52 percent), or £68m. a year, was to come in planned public investment, the rest, £440m. or £62m. a year, in projected private investment. Total cash outlay in 1958–61 had averaged £86m. a year, of which £38m. (or 44 percent) had been in the public sector and £48m. in the private sector. The Plan thus required a substantial increase in both sectors over the rates achieved in 1958–61. In 1962–3, however, public investment had already reached an annual rate of £68m., while private investment had fallen to £35m.; the Plan targets thus required all the additional effort to come from the private sector.

Finance for planned investment in the public sector was to come from current budget surpluses estimated at £100m. (or 21 percent of the total); from domestic loans (£26m. or 5 percent) and from external grants and loans to the value of £239m. (or 50 percent); making a total of £365, or 76 per cent of the full requirement. The shortfall of

£110m. was to be covered, in equal proportions, by Central Bank or deficit financing, and by taxation on cocoa exports, in the event of an increase in their price over that assumed in the Plan; failing that, investment was to be trimmed back accordingly.

The sectoral distribution of planned public investment under the Seven-Year Plan, together with the planned distribution in the discarded Five-Year Plan and the distribution actually achieved during 1959–63, are shown in Table 4.1. The most striking difference is in the allocation to agriculture and industry, which under the Seven-Year Plan

Table 4.1 Differences in the sectoral allocations in public investment between the Five-Year and Seven-Year Plans. (annual average)

	Seven-Year Plan (1964–1970) Proposed [1]		Five-Year Plan (small coat) Proposed		Public Investment (1959–1963) Actual [2]	
	(£m.)	(%)	(£m.)	(%)	(£m.)	(%)
Agriculture	10.3	(15)	2.1	(8)	3.8	(7)
Manufacturing and Mining	16.5	(24)	3.2	(12)	10.7	(20)
Infrastructure and Public Services	18.6	(27)	8.2	(31)	18.2	(34)
Education	9.6	(14)	2.9	(11)	4.8	(9)
Health, Social Service and Housing	9.5	(14)	5.0	(19)	7.0	(13)
General Government	3.5	(5)	5.0	(19)	9.1	(17)
Total	68.0	(100)	26.4	(100)	53.6	(100)

Notes: 1. Sectoral shares exclude annual contingency provision of £3.6m.

2. Includes capital contribution for Volta Project (£2m. annually).

Sources: 1. **Seven-Year Plan**, Table 2.4; supplemented by information derived from the sectoral projections in the plan.

2. See also Statistical Appendix.

accounted for 39 percent, compared with 20 percent proposed, and 27 percent actually invested, during 1959–63. The most significant reductions in the Seven-Year Plan were in the relative allocations for housing and social services, and for general government services.

The increased allocations to agriculture and industry reflect the renewed determination to shift resources into immediately 'productive' investments. They also show the switch of emphasis from support services to the private sector to direct government involvement in production: about 50 percent of capital allocated to agriculture, and more than 75 percent to industry, were destined respectively for state farm and industrial enterprises.

Despite the Plan's emphasis on state enterprise, and the substantial allocation of investment funds, the total contribution of state industries and farms to output was not expected to be very large: by 1970 they were planned to account for less than one-fifth of the additional industrial output and for just under one-third of the additional agricultural output. Even so, these expectations were unlikely to be fulfilled.

The difficulties encountered by the IDC in its industrial operations in the 'fifties should have been taken as a warning of the difficulties to be faced during the Seven-Year Plan. In his analysis of IDC-operated or -controlled enterprises, Killick[2] drew attention to four special problem areas: (1) inadequacy of prior investigation; (2) uncertainty of raw material supplies; (3) a deficiency of working capital; and (4) lack of personnel and poor management. There was little reason for believing at the start of the Seven-Year Plan that these problems would henceforth be resolved more successfully. Although naturally some improvements could be expected as a result of the accumulating experience of running public industries, the quickening pace of expansion in state enterprises would exacerbate the shortage of suitable technical, professional, and managerial personnel.

Although the state farms were expected to contribute no more than a third of additional agricultural output, in one respect their significance was greater than this figure suggests. The projected rate of increase in the output of domestic food crops was put at 4.5 percent per year, representing a 50 percent improvement on the rate of increase achieved in 1955–62; most of this was expected to come from the state farms. The planners felt that it would take a long time before peasant farming could be modernised sufficiently for output per man to increase much above the then current rates. This judgement may have been correct, but there was no evidence that the state farms could do much better in the short run. The first state farm had been set up only in 1961; the government had as yet little experience of running them. Moreover, state farms were intended to pioneer a variety of new techniques, such as large-scale mechanised farming, to be responsible for opening up new land for agriculture, and to introduce new crops, which first had to be tested in Ghanaian conditions, and for which markets had to be found. The big allocation to state farms within the total public sector investment allocation for agriculture was, therefore, a major gamble.

The allocation for support services to private farmers, at £2.4m. a year, remained unchanged from its level in the 1950s, despite the planners' recognition that in the past this had not been adequate. Instead of increasing the allocation, the Plan proposed to remedy the previous deficiency by requiring that more of the government's efforts should go to activities designed specifically to raise agricultural production.

In addition to the support services to private agriculture and industry, the planners envisaged three other forms of government help. The first was the expanded state industries programme itself: it was supposed to provide a nucleus of industrial enterprises around which local entrepreneurs could establish themselves, either as suppliers of services and components, or as users of semi-finished products and by-products. More generally, state industries were to provide a training-ground for an industrial labour force and help develop management skills, both of which would eventually be useful to private industry. The second provision, as in the case of the previous plans, was additional public sector investment in infrastructure and general service; but this time the Plan explicitly recognised the need for a selective approach, with priority for projects serving the specific needs of designated productive activities. The third provision was protection against competition from imports; both general protection by way of direct controls or high duties on imported consumer goods (forced on Ghana in any case by the foreign exchange scarcity), and specific protection to encourage domestic production of particular commodities.

The impact of these provisions could be no more than limited. The first was the most uncertain; in any event it could work only in the long term. The second was much more promising; and yet, on the experience of the past, it was doubtful whether Plan provisions on selectivity in the choice of projects would be realised. The third was double-edged: protection offered through import controls and other measures could provide some inducement, for example, through the producer's ability to raise prices to give an adequate profit; but then import controls, unless skilfully managed, could also handicap growing concerns, particularly if foreign exchange was very scarce. In general, the planners were too ready to assume that public investment necessarily stimulated private sector activity; they appear to have dismissed the possibility that a high level of public investment could of itself discourage private investment.

One of the more curious features of the Plan was the optimistic assessment (when it came to setting private output targets) of the entrepreneurial capacity of Ghanaians; this flatly contradicted the case made for supporting state farms and industries, which stressed the inadequacies of Ghanaian entrepreneurs:

> For the next twenty years their savings would continue to flow predominantly into real estate, education, trading and farming. These would be the types of investment the management of which would be within their entrepreneurial competence. Manufacturing and similar enterprise, with their problems of large-scale labour control, machine running and maintenance, stock control, accounting and other procedures. . . all these would clearly lie beyond their entrepreneurial horizon. . . Another type of investor is needed to supplement the existing type and to carry the main burden for bringing about those structural changes which are essential to the long-run development of the economy but which would not otherwise occur. The state itself is pre-eminently suited for this role.[3]

And yet, this traditional entrepreneur was expected to contribute 60 percent of the additional output in modern manufacturing and in construction, with the other 40 percent divided equally between state and expatriate enterprise.

One of the key considerations in the Seven-Year Plan was Ghana's weak external payments situation. But achievement of production targets and improvement in the balance of payments were intimately related: failure to achieve the planned growth rate in output, especially of food for domestic consumption and local processing, and of manufactured consumer goods which could displace some part of current consumer imports, would have contributed to a further deterioration in Ghana's external position; conversely, failure to improve the foreign exchange situation would have jeopardised growth. The planners had allowed for extremely small margins within which to manage the foreign exchange account. Annual imports were planned to increase from £152m. in 1960–62, to £231m. in 1970. This represented a fall, as a percentage of GDP, from a level of 30 per cent in 1960–62 to 26.5 percent in 1970. Exports were expected to increase, over the same period, from £122m. to £195m., bringing the current deficit up from £30m. to £36m. or, as a percentage of GDP, down from 6 percent to 2.2 percent. The import projections were based on an overall increase of 60 percent in the value of food imports (a realistically safe figure) and an increase of only 12.5 percent in other consumer imports – a not unrealistic figure to assume provided that import controls were efficiently applied, and in view of the fact that the main import items to have expanded since the mid-1950s were intermediate and capital goods. The Plan assumed also a zero net increase in expenditure on 'invisibles', such as insurance, travel and remittance of dividends; this assumption was entirely unfounded. Export projections were based on the assumption of constant cocoa prices, over the life of the Plan, an assumption which was on the cautious side, given that the base was a period of depressed prices.

On the capital account side, the Plan envisaged an inflow of funds for financing private sector investment of around £100m., equivalent to 11 percent of total projected private cash investment, and a further net inflow, for use in the public sector, of £239m. Of the £100m. in private investment, £45m. had already been secured for the Kaiser (or VALCO) aluminium smelter. A further £55m., or £8m. a year, thus remained to be secured. The planners claimed an inflow of overseas funds for direct investment of £5m. a year during 1958–62; but this claim is not borne out by government balance of payments estimates, where a figure of £0.5m. net is recorded. In 1963 this had risen to £3.7m.; even so there was still a considerable leeway to be made up to reach the level projected in the Plan.

The expected dependence of public investment on foreign loans is striking. As a proportion of total public investment the Seven-Year Plan figure for foreign credit was two-and-half times bigger than the expected Five-Year Plan figure, and in absolute terms as much as seven times bigger. Yet there was a good chance that Ghana would be able to raise the entire sum. Already before the Plan was published, loans and credits valued at £100m. had been negotiated (although not all of them had been signed when the Plan estimates were made). A further £20m. remained outstanding from the Volta loan, leaving a balance of £119m. still to be raised. However, the planners had made their calculation of external capital needs on the assumption that new credits would be offered on concessionary interest rates and with long maturities, to avoid, in particular, the bunching of repayments towards, or immediately after, the end of the Plan. This assumption was still realistic (although only just) at the time the calculations were made; but it was invalid by the time the Plan was launched. In 1963 alone Ghana signed medium-term credits of £44m., most of which carried interest rates of over 5 percent and were to mature before 1970. By March 1964, the Plan estimate for debt-servicing during 1964–70 had risen from £55m. to over £100m. If Ghana had tried to compensate for this by raising further medium-term credits in the course of the Plan, the servicing problem would merely have been postponed into the early 1970s. Thus, even if all the plan assumptions and projections of output and the balance of payments for the entire period of the Plan proved correct, recourse to medium-term credits for financing planned public sector investment was leading Ghana into a serious debt trap.

3. The relationship between public investment, state enterprise and external finance.

In the period when the Seven-Year Plan was being prepared, that is between the setting of the planning guidelines in early 1962 and the launching of the Plan in early 1964, there was no pause for reorientation similar to the pause before the launching of the Five-Year Plan. Ministries were left to get on with the implementation of programmes and projects included in the officially defunct Five-Year Plan, while at the same time new projects anticipating the next plan were also launched, many of them for no other reason than that external credits were available to finance them. Although the Seven-Year Plan guidelines called for a major reorientation towards direct public investment in agricultural and industrial production, in the two years before the plan was launched a total of £48m. a year (or 70 percent), out of an annual public investment budget of £68m., was devoted to other uses, more than the annual rate of investment in all sectors in the four previous years. In the first two years after the plan was launched (i.e. 1963–4) the overall annual rate for public investment shot up to £108m.; with £39m. (or 36 percent) going into agriculture and industry and £69m. divided between all other sectors.

Figures for the four-year period from 1962 to 1965 are shown in Table 4.2, together with comparable figures for the previous eight years. For 1962–5 the annual public investment rate worked out at £87.5m., with one-third going to agriculture and industry, and the rest on all other sectors. This compared with investment rates of £38m. and £19m. (with the share of agriculture and industry at 24 percent and 11 percent) in the periods 1958–61 and 1954–7 respectively.

The figures in the table also bring out the rapid rise to prominence after 1961 of state enterprise. In 1958–61 investment in state enterprise had accounted for only 5 percent of the total, and for 20 percent of total public spending on agriculture and industry, with a large part of the remaining 80 percent going into a few large private state joint ventures. By the end of 1961 the number of state enterprises (excluding public utilities, trading and marketing corporations, and financial institutions) numbered nineteen: two pioneer state farms; the gold mines bought from private companies in 1960; and a handful of manufacturing and service industries set up or taken over by the Industrial Development Corporation since its founding in 1951.[4] In the period 1962–5, £27m. a year went into state enterprises, nearly all in the agricultural and industrial sectors; moreover, state industries now accounted for 90 percent of total public investment in these sectors, with the remainder going on support services to the private sector. Out of the total of £27m. a year, some £22m. a year was used to start new enterprises: £5m. divided equally between the State Farms Corporation and the State Fishing Corporation, with most of the remaining £17m. going on new industrial ventures.

The state farms programmes was the single most important public enterprise venture in 1962–5. From their pioneering beginnings in the late 1950s, state farms had by 1965 become the spearhead of what was intended to be a major new attack on Ghana's agricultural problems. At the peak of the programme in 1965, the State Farms Corporation, jointly with the United Ghana Farmers' Co-operative Council and the Workers' Brigade, controlled sixty-nine separate farms, with a total land area of 700,000 acres (of which about 100,000 were under cultivation), the agricultural extension service, and a string of processing plants and machinery service and hire stations. However, since the acreage under cultivation accounted for less than 5 percent of the Ghanaian total, the state farms could make little impact on the overall supply of food crops. They did, all the same, absorb a very large slice of public spending on agriculture, available machinery (owning between them some 1,500 tractors alone) and, through control over the extension services, much of the skilled agricultural manpower previously available for helping the peasant cultivator. Moreover, the farms were generally badly managed and made a substantial overall financial loss throughout the period.

Table 4.2 The importance of public investment in agriculture and industry, and in state enterprises in relation to external capital, 1954–1957, 1958–1961, 1962–1965.

	1954 – 57		1958 – 61 (annual averages)		1962 – 65	
	(£m.)	(%)	(£m.)	(%)	(£m.)	(%)
Total public domestic investment	19.0		38.0		87.0	
of which: state enterprises	0.5	(3)	2.0	(5)	27.0	(31)
Total public investment in agriculture & industry (annual value and as a % of total investment)	2.1	(11)	9.1	(24)	30.0	(34)
of which: state enterprises	0.4	(20)	1.8	(20)	27.0	(90)
Sources of finance						
recurrent budget [1]	19.6	(103)	14.7	(39)	16.7	(19)
reserves [2]	-2.8	(-15)	17.2[3]	(45)	18.3	(21)
external medium & long-term capital (net)	0.5	(3)	6.1	(16)	27.0[4]	(31)
other domestic & external	1.7[5]	(9)	-	(-)	25.0[6]	(29)
External capital for state enterprises in agriculture and industry	-	(-)	0.2[7]	(10)	10.0	(39)

Notes:
1. Surplus of central government current revenue over current expenditure allocated to public sector investment, including both government and public corporations.
2. A minus sign indicates increase (i.e. an investment in foreign securities).
3. Excludes drawings on reserves for financing aid to Mali and Guinea.
4. cf. gross disbursements of £31.1m. a year (see Table 3.2)
5. Loan from the accumulated reserves of the Cocoa Marketing Board.
6. Comprises short-term foreign credits, payment arrears, and bilateral trade balances (total £5m.–£10m.); short-term loans from commercial banks and Post Office Savings Bank; loans from Central Bank (deficit financing).
7. Rough Estimate.

Sources: See Statistical Appendix.

Between 1962 and 1965 thirteen new state industrial enterprises were completed, and work on another nineteen was under way.[5] Some of these industries had long been considered desirable; plans for cement, leather tanning and sugar had been proposed as far back as 1951. Some others, such as glass and canned fruit and vegetables, were considered suitable by Lewis in 1953 (see Ch.2). Still others, including the steel mill and meat products factories, appeared in the Five-Year Plan and had been assessed as viable at the time. But the final list included also some items which Lewis had either turned down or approved only with reservation (such as cocoa products and textiles) and others whose potential viability in principle and under ideal conditions had been established, but which had not been subjected to a full independent technical and economic appraisal (such as cement and sugar). The others appeared on the final list either because they were 'sold' by interested suppliers, or thought of (often on the spur of the moment) by Nkrumah or one of his ministers or confidants. And even in those cases where a particular plant might have been viable in Ghanaian conditions, viability was often jeopardised either by poor management, or by the failure to consider the plant in the context of other measures; the viability of the glass works, for instance, was undermined by the massive purchase of East European glass and bottles under a trade agreement just at the time when the glass works came into full production. Or again, planning was inept in respect of plant location, scale, and design, and based on poor information concerning availability of raw materials, market requirements and so on. While it is extremely difficult to assess the 'intrinsic worth' of the enterprises initiated during the period, the list of blunders committed in planning, execution, or management stands as an indictment of the Ghana government as well as the foreign suppliers and contractors, whether private or public, with whom it had dealings (see Section 4,iii).

All but one of the enterprises initiated in 1962–5 involved credit agreements with foreign suppliers and contractors. Foreign credits nonetheless covered only just over 40 percent of the total capital costs which were actually incurred (or 39 percent if the cost of the state farms is included). However, taking into account the 'pipeline' on projects nearing completion at the time of the 1966 coup, about 50 percent of the total capital cost of state industries launched after 1961 was financed with medium-term private supplier or Eastern government credits.

Overall, such credits covered 30 percent of all Ghanaian public investment during 1962–5; this compares with 16 percent in 1958–61 and only 3 percent in 1954–7. In 1954–7 recurrent revenue surpluses were big enough to cover the entire capital needs of the public sector. By 1958–61 this figure had fallen to 39 percent, and by 1962 to as low as 19 percent. Initially, the shortfall was made up by running down reserves, and only to a smaller extent by external credits; in 1958–61 reserves still financed 45 percent of public investment. During 1962–5, however, reserves were exhausted; after 1963 the financial shortfall was made up entirely by medium-term external credits, as well as by short-term external credits and internal deficit financing, in almost equal proportions.

The role played by external medium-term credits (i.e. all Ghana's credits except those for the Volta Project, which were long-term) in sustaining the high public investment rate after 1961 was rather more ambiguous than the ratio of credits to total investment seems to suggest. This gives the impression that credits allowed Ghana to sustain a given, high rate of investment. In reality, the availability of credits itself pushed up the investment rate above the level originally set by the planners. Because the government was conscious that Ghana lacked not only financial resources, but also the capacity to initiate, prepare, appraise, implement, and manage projects in the industrial field, it entered into arrangements with expert suppliers of plant and machinery which could allow Ghana to implement a larger programme. However, easy access to credit made Ghana accept projects which had not previously appeared in the programmes of ministries or public corporations, for no better reasons than that credit was available. Since these credits normally covered only a part of the total cost of plant and equipment or construction work, Ghana's own funds were diverted from other planned uses. In succumbing to the temptation to launch new projects partly financed from credit, and at the same time attempting to implement all the other projects previously planned, Ghana had to resort to short-term foreign and Central Bank borrowing – forms of finance still more dangerous to its economic health than medium-term credits.

4. External credits: origins, types, terms and uses

i) Official aid from the West

Between independence and the end of 1961 Ghana's one major aid success with Western governments and international financial institutions was the Volta loan agreement. During 1962–5 the first stage of the project, comprising the Akosombo dam and hydro-electric station, was completed, with the first generators coming into service in late 1965. Out of a total of £35m. available in aid, only £23m. was needed for this stage. In addition to the Volta loans, Ghana obtained one export credit of £2.2m. from the British government for the purchase of commercial vessels, and one for £1.8m. from the German Federal Republic for a bridge over the Lower Volta on the road linking Ghana, Togo, Dahomey, and Nigeria. That made up the entire disbursement of official aid up to the overthrow of Nkrumah; a total of £27m., shared between the World Bank (50 percent), the United States (25 percent), Britain (17 percent), and Germany (8 percent).

Until 1961, while looking for aid, Ghana had been quite able to get by on its own resources. During 1961, particularly in view of Nkrumah's determination to continue with his ambitious policies, the need for external capital became urgent. Nkrumah was, however, slow to recognise the urgency, since at that time he was about to sign the Volta agreement and, moreover, there appeared to be no shortage of offers of credit from East European countries and Western contractors and capital goods exporters. His attitude caused considerable concern among those officials who recognised the danger of relying almost exclusively on medium-term credit. They urged a determined drive to secure more loans on the sort of terms being offered for the Volta Project, which meant, in practice, a renewed effort to raise loans from Western governments. Nkrumah was eventually persuaded by them of the necessity of this course of action if his investment programme was to be carried through.

While Ghana had received, and continued to receive, technical assistance from many Western governments, it had failed to attract capital aid or to develop close links with potential donors, other than in the context of the Volta negotiations. These negotiations involved mainly the World Bank, and on the American side the Export-Import Bank, rather than the main agency responsible for capital aid, the Development Loan Fund (absorbed into the new AID during 1961). The lack of on-going capital aid programmes proved a considerable handicap when it came to raising aid in the wake of the 1961 balance of payments crisis. It is one of the characteristics of aid that patterns established as a result of a response to some particular set of events tend to persist, often long after the original rationale has disappeared. Major inter-country reallocations in a donor's aid budget tend to come infrequently, and once a country receives assistance it can usually count on support continuing for a number of years, with the level of support

Table 4.3 Foreign grants, loans and credits extended to Ghana : agreements and gross disbursements 1950–1970[1]

(£m.)

	Agreements negotiated[2]					Gross disbursements				
	Volta project	Other Western aid	Suppliers' Credits	Eastern loans	Total	Volta project	Other Western aid	Suppliers' Credits	Eastern loans	Total
Total 1950–57	0.2	2.0			2.2	0.2	3.3			3.5
1958										
1959			0.7		0.7		0.2	0.9		1.1
1960			7.9	2.4	10.3		0.2	10.8	1.0	12.0
1961	30.0		9.0	4.3	43.3			9.4	2.0	11.4
Total 1958–61	30.0		17.6	6.7	54.3		0.4	21.1	3.0	24.5
1962	5.0		16.8	10.0	31.8	3.0		8.4	4.0	15.4
1963		4.0	42.4	9.9	56.3	5.1		21.5	5.0	31.6
1964			39.5	9.1	48.6	7.9	1.0	18.1	7.0	34.0
1965			48.2	3.3	51.5	7.0	3.0	23.5	10.0	43.5
Total 1962–65	5.0	4.0	146.9	32.3	188.2	23.0	4.0	71.5	26.0	124.5
1966		6.3			6.3	4.8	4.2	15.3	5.0	29.3
1967		18.8			18.8		3.9	5.0	4.0	12.9
1968		25.9			25.9		14.2			14.2
1969		18.7			18.7		18.8			18.8
Total 1966–69		69.7			69.7	4.8	41.1	20.3	9.0	75.1
Grand total	35.2	75.7	164.5	39.0	314.4	28.0	48.8	112.9	38.0	227.7
(1970	–		n.a.	n.a.		n.a.	24.0	n.a.	n.a.	24.0)

Notes: 1. Value of agreements and disbursements after devaluation of the Cedi in mid-1967 arrived at by converting at the pre-devaluation exchange-rate, i.e. £1 = N¢2.

2. Excludes general technical assistance agreements. No record exists of the original agreement in respect of a number of suppliers' credits; hence the value of agreements negotiated is less than actual disbursements in the period 1958–61. The table excludes also CD&W commitments made prior to 1950; all disbursements since 1950 are, however, included.

3. The timing of disbursements is approximate only.

Sources: See Statistical Appendix.

changing only by a little from year to year unless special circumstances warrant a major upward or downward change. Similarly, once a country has been left out, it is not easily reabsorbed into the mainstream of aid. By missing the current at around independence, partly through circumstances and partly through its own lack of endeavour, Ghana remained effectively stranded. This was particularly unfortunate since the period just prior to 1962 saw a very rapid expansion in Western aid commitments.

By the end of 1961, the conditions in which Ghana's aid merits had earlier been assessed, and accorded a low priority, had clearly changed. The balance of payments crisis in itself provided sufficient ground for a positive reaction from donors to Ghana's new demands. Similar balance of payments crises in India and Pakistan, and more recently in Tunisia, following the exhaustion of foreign reserves which they had accumulated before independence, had brought a speedy response from the United States and, in some cases following US pressure, from other governments. In Ghana's case, however, there was no response.

A number of reasons, superficially quite plausible, have been advanced to explain this lack of interest on the part of Western governments. The first of these was that relations between Ghana and both Britain and the United States -- which, together with the German Federal Republic were the most likely countries to have come to Ghana's aid – were too strained for them to wish to make the required gesture of support. But this could not have been important, since in 1961–2 relations had not yet deteriorated to the point where co-operation on aid was impossible; and in any case, the United States had not refrained from providing substantial quantities of aid to, for instance, Indonesia, a country with which political relations had reached a very low ebb. Another reason put forward was Western dislike of Ghana's authoritarian, one-party system; but again, this did not prevent the United States from giving aid to Taiwan and South Korea, or Britain from giving aid to Jordan, or both from giving aid to Libya. Ghana's espousal of 'socialism' and its overtures to the East, including East Germany, probably disqualified it then from West German capital aid; but both Britain and America had given substantial aid to Yugoslavia, and to many countries which maintained friendly relations with Russia or received its aid, including most notably India. Other reasons which were produced had, yet again, not disqualified other countries from either British or American aid; recourse to supplier credit and a strong emphasis on state enterprise had, for example, not disqualified either India or Turkey; and economic mismanagement had not disqualified even Indonesia.

If all these reasons are put together they do, however, seem to add up to a sufficiently persuasive explanation as to why Ghana did not obtain the support it sought. And yet, if either Britain or America had considered Ghana important, for strategic, political, or commercial reasons, none of these reasons, singly or in combination, would have stood in the way of aid. Indeed, many of them – for instance, Ghana's turning to the East, its recourse to suppliers' credits or Eastern aid, its emphasis on state enterprise and control, and even its economic mismanagement – would have been adduced as reasons for an aid presence, rather than an aid boycott. But Ghana's only real importance to the West was its dominant position in the world cocoa market; as long as cocoa supplies were not threatened – and there was no reason to suppose that Ghana could dispose of its crop if it chose to deny supplies to the West – Ghana's internal and international behaviour was of no major consequence. A number of British companies had substantial stakes in Ghana, but the total stake was very small. The United States had only negligible interests, and this was the case too for most European countries. Politically and strategically Ghana's friendship was useful, but its hostility could have been no more than a nuisance, unless the country became a major and effective base for subversion in Africa, and even this would not have ranked as very important. Ghana's insignificance, particularly to the United States, was in the end the most important contributory factor to Ghana's lack of success in raising Western aid in 1961–2.

Ghana continued to make some efforts to obtain aid, though rather half-heartedly, and in 1963 managed to arrange two small credits. The first was for £2.2m. for eleven years, under a new British scheme which sought to link the provision of overseas aid to assistance to British firms with excess capacity. The second was for £1.8m. for fifteen years, under a German scheme to help African regional development. When the Seven-Year Plan was published in 1964, efforts to attract aid were renewed; but by that time few countries were prepared to show an interest, even in discussions. Political relations with Britain and America had deteriorated sharply, with Britain, in particular, subjected to an increasing barrage of abuse, culminating in Nkrumah's break in diplomatic relations over the Rhodesian issue. Moreover, at the time of the publication of Ghana's Seven-Year Plan, Britain's balance of payments difficulties were having an adverse effect on aid spending; even with a more favourable political climate the constraints on the British aid budget would have made it difficult to set aside more than token sums towards Ghana's Plan. The timing of the Seven-Year Plan was also inauspicious where American aid was concerned. In 1962–3 the US aid budget had been subjected to the strongest attack from Congress yet. The Administration had responded to congressional criticisms by setting up an independent committee to review the entire aid programme. The committee's report (the Clay Report), which came out in 1963, recommended substantial reductions and greater selectivity in the choice of new aid schemes where Africa was concerned. Moreover, the general trend in US aid policy, particularly for countries in which US strategic interests were not paramount, was towards much stricter surveillance of recipient economic policies and a strong preference for those recipients whose development performance was judged to be sound. In 1962 Ghana had been placed in the 'limited programme', or lowest priority, category. From 1963, even the until then quite substantial technical assistance programme was reduced. By 1965, the American presence had been reduced to a minimum, sufficient only to show some evidence of US goodwill towards the people of the country, despite US 'displeasure' with the Nkrumah government; the US AID office in Accra was in fact scheduled to close at the end of the US 1965–6 fiscal year.

In terms of its actual overall contribution to Ghana's development under Nkrumah, the impact of Western aid must, therefore, be judged largely in terms of the Volta Project. In terms of the specific objectives of the project agreement as negotiated, Volta has fully come up to expectations. However, in terms of its general contribution to the economy, its success has been no more than modest. Opinion is still divided as to whether the massive investment was really justified by the return obtained. The World Bank itself has had second thoughts, and it seems likely that on the criteria which have come into greater prominence since the project was completed – such as the contribution of investment to employment or income distribution, in addition to its financial return – the project would not have been sanctioned. This does not mean that the project was ill-advised, but it does suggest that the funds put into it might have been used to better effect in other ventures – as indeed the Ghana Ministry of Finance had long claimed.

The importance of Western aid to Ghana's development, and more particularly to its external debt predicament, cannot be judged, however, purely in terms of its actual contribution; some account must also be taken of the effect its failure to materialise in greater quantities may have had. It would be fruitless, of course, to draw precise conclusions from what must be, by its very nature, conjecture. One conclusion is, nevertheless, inescapable: it is that Ghana's failure to attract aid in the immediate aftermath of the 1961 balance of payments crisis had a particularly harmful effect because aid could have benefitted Ghana in at least three ways. First, at least some of the projects financed by supplier credits or short-term borrowing would have been financed by long-term loans, some of them at very low interest. This would have ensured, at the same time, a higher standard of planning and control over contractors, and, in some cases also, a lower net cost (see below, Section 4,iii). There is, of course, always the possibility that aid would merely have added to the total volume of spending, rather than have replaced one form of finance for another, with a constant number of projects. But this seems unlikely if considered in relation to the next two points. Second, if more donors had been actively involved and had committed public funds towards Ghana's development, particularly if Britain had been among these, it is highly probable that the danger of providing government guarantees for a large number of supplier credits would have been noted and effective action taken earlier (see Section 4,iii). Third, the active interest of donors, particularly the pressure of a major US AID mission, would have strengthened the hand of those Ghanaian officials who wished to impose some order and restraint on public investment. In addition, donor scrutiny of projects, advice and help with feasibility studies, insistence on the use of reputable consultants (with a measure of control over their work), and technical assistance provided in connection with projects, would inevitably have helped to avoid some of the grossest abuses and deceits, as well as incompetence, associated with many of the projects financed by medium-term credits from both East and West.

No donor could have expected an easy time in Ghana; but, on the basis of some of the results achieved in limited areas of technical assistance – such as the American extension service programme – the effort need not have been futile. Correspondingly, some of the mistakes made by Ghana in the 1962–5 period would have been forestalled.

ii) Private foreign investment

It was one of the features of Ghana's attitude after 1961, restated at the time of the launching of the Seven-Year Plan, that the pursuit of socialism and the emphasis on state enterprise should not preclude the private sector, domestic and foreign, making an important contribution. Indeed, the Plan objectives had been based on an investment contribution from the private sector of almost one-half of the total. Ghana not only continued to operate its incentive schemes for private foreign investment, but substantially increased them through the 1963 Capital Investments Act. However, many of the restrictive measures (introduced in 1961–2 and again in 1965), within which the private sector as a whole had to operate, and the hostile propaganda directed by Nkrumah and senior CPP colleagues against capitalism, Western interests, and 'bourgeois exploitation' were not conducive to new investment in the country.

Actual private foreign investment in 1962–5, contrary to what might have been expected, averaged £7m. net a year, far better than the rate achieved over any other four-year period since at least 1950. Moreover, the annual rate over the period itself accelerated, and by 1964–5 exceeded the rate needed to achieve the planned contribution over the life of the Seven-Year Plan. However, about half of this investment, and a much higher proportion in 1965, were financed out of retained profits. This feature was encouraged, or made necessary, by the restrictions imposed on profit remittance and repatriation of capital, which were progressively tightened until by 1965 it was impossible legally to transfer any funds out of Ghana. The profits which were earned by private foreign concerns were also artificially swollen by heavy protection, import controls and inflation, at least until 1965, by which time the acute shortage of foreign exchange itself seriously hampered their operations. Because of this, the higher rate of investment may well have proved temporary, with a return to more normal levels of protection and more freely available foreign exchange reducing both profits and the attaction of reinvestment of profits in Ghana over their remittance. Also, some of the investments made in the period reflected commitments entered into before 1962, particularly those in joint private state ventures (most notably a brewery, and bottling and aluminium works); after 1962 only three more joint venture agreements were concluded, for a television and two motor vehicle assembly plants.

Although the profitability of some private or private/state ventures started in 1962–5 depended initially on either generous government concessions or protection, the majority appeared to be capable of sustaining (and indeed did sustain) themselves in less artificial conditions. Moreover, the period of restrictions on profit remittance, as well as the control over overseas transfer of commercial bank deposits, did force some of the established foreign concerns, which normally looked elsewhere for a profitable investment of surplus funds (e.g. through their parent companies), to consider local alternatives; this set a precedent which some of the concerns found it profitable to follow later. Foreign private investment in 1962--5 did, therefore, make both a short-term and a long-term contribution to Ghana's economy. However, there was also a price to be paid, particularly in the short to medium term. In the short term, some of the success of foreign concerns was gained at the expense of small Ghanaian enterprises. First, large foreign concerns and joint state private enterprises found it much easier to be exempted from, or get round, restrictions and regulations imposed by the government. This was particularly evident in the relative ease (until late 1965) with which they managed to obtain import licences; the small indigenous entrepreneur was in a much more vulnerable position and suffered accordingly. Second, the build-up of short-term liabilities by the requirement to purchase even essential imports on 180-day credit, and the even more substantial build-up of profits and other payments for transfer overseas during the period of restriction or ban on such remittances, added seriously to Ghana's foreign exchange liabilities in the immediate post-Nkrumah period.

iii) Supplier credits and East European loans

Between 1959 and 1965, the years of the first and last medium-term credit agreements, a total of 215–220 (183 after 1961) such contracts were signed, to a value of around £250m. Of this, £203m. (or £180m. on contracts signed after 1961) represented the actual credit portion (i.e. excluding down payments made by Ghana); £164m. from private Western companies, and £39m. from Eastern governments or state corporations. Out of the total of £203m. of credit contracted, only £151m. was actually used -- £113m. from the West and £38m. from the East. Official balance of payments figures show that £98m. was 'used' during 1962–5; but including equipment and work already in the pipeline, the effective figure for credits 'used' then rises to £126m., or 84 percent of the overall total of £151m.

The peak period for new agreements with Western suppliers was 1963--4, even though the value of contracts signed in 1965 exceeded that in any previous year. Seven of the twenty contracts signed in 1965 (or three-quarters of the total credit value) were with the Drivici group (based in Germany and Switzerland), and most of these were either cancelled or suspended after the 1966 coup. By this time Ghana's creditworthiness had declined to the point where insurance cover for credits could no longer be easily arranged, and without insurance, credit offers virtually dried up – the Drivici Group was one of the few remaining concerns still prepared to extend large credits, in part because Drivici himself appears to have attained a special position of trust and influence with Nkrumah.

The peak period for East European credit agreements was reached earlier, in 1962–3. Relations with Russia, in particular, became strained during 1964; the Russians appear to have become irritated with Nkrumah and to have had second thoughts about the value of their commitment to Ghana. Ghanaian officials had also become frustrated by the difficulties raised by the Russians in some of the project negotiations, and one agreement at least was abandoned after it had already been initialled. In the end, the £30m. aid agreement reached with Russia in 1960 was only about half-fulfilled. In 1965, the only two contracts of significance to be negotiated were with China, which had by then become one of the few remaining sources of credit to which Nkrumah could turn.

In all, over twenty countries in both East and West were involved in supplier credit agreements. The single most important creditor country was Britain, with 31 percent (by value) of all credits which were taken up. West Germany was next with 24 percent, followed a long way behind by Russia (9 percent), the Netherlands (8 percent), Czechoslovakia (5 percent), France and Yugoslavia (4 percent each), Japan (3 percent), and Poland (2 percent); between them these nine countries accounted for 90 percent of the total. Britain alone accounted for 44 percent of the total value of *private* supplier credits which were used.

The majority of private credits were guaranteed against default on repayment on dates due; either direct by the governments of the suppliers, as in the case of Britain, where the guarantor was the Export Credits Guarantee Department (ECGD) of the then Board of Trade, or by government-appointed agencies, as in the case of West Germany, where the Hermes Credit Insurance Company acted as a guarantor on behalf of, and under instruction from, the German Government, or, in the case of the Netherlands and France, by the state-controlled corporations NCM[6] and COFACE.[7] These guarantees, for which varying premiums were charged according to the credit standing of the recipient concerned, usually covered all but a small part of the total credit (including interest). The guarantees were offered mainly to encourage exports of costly equipment and capital goods for commercial (and exceptionally for 'national interest') reasons, and the use to which these were put was usually of no particular concern to the guarantor agencies, as long as the purchaser's credit standing remained good. In Ghana's case, all the credits which were guaranteed were made either to the government or to public corporations; they thus all carried an implicit Ghana government guarantee. In this case, therefore, the credit standing of the particular concerns taking up the credits was of little interest to the creditor governments; their main concern was with the creditworthiness of the country, and it is on this that they based the premiums and conditions on which guarantees were made available.

Cover remained available throughout the 1962–5 period, despite Ghana's rapidly deteriorating balance of payments and budgetary position, the exhaustion of reserves, and the rapid accumulation of short-term credits. ECGD cover remained available on a restricted basis from 1961, following Ghana's balance of payments crisis; the 'restrictions' included higher insurance premiums and a limit on ECGD's overall liability. Although cover could not be secured for some contracts – a civil engineering contract was lost in 1964, for instance, because cover could not be arranged – there was nevertheless a rapid build-up in British guaranteed credit up to 1965. More severe restrictions were introduced in that year, leading to a sharp drop in the number of guarantees, and in the number of credit contracts. Britain's experience was repeated in other countries: German guaranteed credits also rose rapidly over the period up to 1965, despite high premiums; on one credit made in 1962, the premium came to 8½ percent of the contract price (paid in this case by the Ghana government rather than, as was usual, by the financing institution or supplier).

The availability of guarantees in a period when Ghana's credit standing was worsening rapidly was a major factor behind the willingness of suppliers to continue offering credit contracts on a massive scale. But it is difficult to understand why guarantees were not withdrawn when it had become clear that Ghana's total debt burden was rapidly reaching an unmanageable level. In 1962, at the time of Ghana's first stand-by credit drawing on the IMF (and with still greater emphasis in 1963 and 1964), the Fund's report had warned of the consequences of accepting supplier credits in large quantities, and had called for a curtailment of such credits to the most urgent projects for which no other finance could be raised. However, guaranteeing agencies appear to have waited until Ghana actually got into arrears on some of its payments before effectively limiting the number of new guarantee issues.

One of the less desirable features of the credits guaranteed was the hardness of the terms, in respect both of interest charged and, still more, length of maturity. Interest rates on private supplier credits, both guaranteed and unguaranteed, ranged from 4 percent to 6½ percent, with a weighted average of 5.3/8 percent (or 5¼ percent on credits signed after 1962). British and French rates were the highest, with a weighted average of just on 5.5/8 percent; West German and Dutch rates were the lowest among the important creditor countries, at 4.7/8 percent and 4½ percent respectively. While these rates were expensive for a country like Ghana, it must be remembered that they did not compare unfavourably with rates charged on official aid loans at that time. Most European countries charged similar rates on official aid loans and private export credits, both being closely linked to the government borrowing rate for equivalent maturities. Britain started offering concessionary rates on aid to independent countries only late in 1963, and even then its softest rate was above 3 percent. German aid for revenue-earning projects continued to carry commercial rates, and that for infrastructure projects rates of between 3 percent and 3½ percent. The only important donor to offer really soft terms – with a large proportion of interest-free loans – was the United States; although in the case of the Volta loan to Ghana its interest rate was close to 4 percent. The typical interest rate on Eastern government loans to Ghana was 2½ percent, with the exception of those on Yugoslav credits (3 percent) and Chinese credits (zero).

However, the true value of goods and services normally supplied under official Western aid contracts was greater than that for items under private supplier or Eastern credits. The true interest charge was thus considerably more favourable than the nominal interest rates suggest. Overcharging on both Western and Eastern supplier credits to Ghana was common. This was made easy as few of the projects financed by such credits were put out to competitive bidding, and Ghana generally lacked the expertise or manpower to make anything but the most obvious checks; in some cases even these were not carried out, through misplaced trust, or administrative muddle, or political pressure on officials, or the outright dishonesty of 'independent' consultants. As a result, second-hand or obsolescent or defective equipment was supplied when the contract price had covered new or up-to-date equipment; work contracted for was not carried out; and feasibility studies or training provisions included in the contracts were not carried out at all, or only perfunctorily. The contract price often 'covered' also the insurance premium payable on the guarantee, and the 'kick-back' or contribution to CPP funds which had become a normal feature of private supplier credit contracts. An overall downward adjustment of 20 percent for over-charging on all private credits would probably be on the conservative side. There is also evidence of deliberate over-charging on Eastern contracts, although its overall extent is more difficult to judge because of the general problem of pricing goods originating from centrally planned economies. However, in the view of the IMF, which took into account price, quality, and value of barter deals involving repayment in Ghana goods, the true value of goods and services supplied from the East was considerably less than the contract price – by at least 25 percent. Taking into account the inflated price on the full contract – including the down payment – Ghana appears to have received goods and services of no more than about 70 percent – 75 percent of the face value of all the credit contracts it accepted.

The weighted average maturity on Western credits was five-and-a-half years, and on Eastern credits seven-and-a-half years. Overall 60 percent of credit maturities fell within the range of three to six years. There was generally little difference between countries, East or West, but Russia – with a third (by value) of its credits maturing over twelve years – was clearly the most 'generous' among the big creditors. At the time, some Western governments offered aid loans mainly for periods similar to those on credits taken up by Ghana; Britain, Germany, and the United States all offered loans for periods of between eight and fifteen years. But their typical aid loans were for periods comparable to those offered to Ghana for the Volta Project, and some were for still longer periods. It was, in effect, the short maturity on the typical supplier and Eastern credits that really distinguished their terms from those on typical Western government aid loans.

A large part of Ghana's debt problem arose, certainly, from its acceptance of credits on terms which were unsuitable to the projects which they financed. The majority of projects – even those basically sound in intention or conception – could not have generated the income or savings in foreign exchange, either within or soon after the period laid down for discharging the full debt-servicing commitment on them. The situation was further complicated by the often inept planning and execution of the projects, with consequent delays, the possibility of which should have been taken into account in setting credit maturities, but normally was not. Nevertheless, Ghana's problems in relation to the credits were more fundamental than that of appropriate terms. In the first place, credits encouraged overspending and generally reduced discipline. Perhaps as much as half the medium-term credit raised was applied to projects which were not even thought of before the credit offer was made; and since these projects did not usually replace projects already planned, but were additional to them, the government found itself pushed into short-term expedients to raise the balance – such as short-term borrowing and deficit financing – which created their own special problems over and above those posed by the terms on which medium-term credits were accepted. In the second place, many of the projects financed with medium-term credits were entirely inappropriate and impoverishing; the hard terms merely emphasised their inappropriateness rather more quickly and dramatically than if the terms had been softer. The only sensible course here would have been not to accept them.

Out of the total of £151m. in medium-term credits used, just under 30 percent went into state enterprises and just over 70 percent into other sectors, particularly for infrastructure and other construction projects and for the purchase of transport equipment. It is extremely difficult to make a precise assessment of the economic value or contribution of the projects to which medium-term credits were applied. Leaving aside for the moment the state industries, a number of projects or capital items can be listed which were, without the slightest doubt, completely unjustified, and whose contribution to the economy was, moreover, negative, when account is taken of their net recurrent costs and drain on skilled manpower and administrative resources. Among the main ones were the Russian atomic reactor and Ilyushin aircraft (£3.5m.); the French-built Tema hotel and Accra airport terminal (£2m.); the British Accra-Tema motorway, VC-10 aircraft, naval frigate (£14m.); the equipment and construction services from various sources for the Trade Fair complex, the OAU conference building, the Nkrumah Ideological Institute and the Takoradi and Kumasi hotels (approximately £18m.); these and various other minor items make a total of nearly £40m. Much of the rest of the £151m. was devoted to investments which were, to a greater or lesser extent, useful; but not all were of any high economic priority and even when they were, their expense or lavishness was often quite unjustified.

The misuse of resources, both domestic and provided on credit, was particularly apparent in the state industries programme. While Ghana must take the main responsibility for the chaos into which this venture had fallen by the time of the coup, the role played here by foreign consultants, contractors, and suppliers was particularly damaging. The state enterprise programme relied to a far greater extent than any other programme on foreign help in identifying, planning, implementing, and managing the various constituent parts. But the help that came from either private Western companies or the state agencies of Eastern countries was not invariably of a high standard; overall performance was certainly marred by many instances of shoddy work, incompetence, inefficiency or irresponsibility. In these instances external intervention or 'co-operation' only complicated an already entangled administrative system and compounded mistakes originating from the Ghanaian side. The variety of problems which arose is illustrated in a sample of state enterprise ventures, one for each of the five major providers of external credit for such projects – West Germany, France, and Britain from the West and Czechoslovakia and Yugoslavia from the East.

The German project in question, one of seven signed with German suppliers, originated in Ghana's understandable wish to maximise its earnings from cocoa by exporting a part of the crop in a processed form. But, as in the case of other projects for which the motive was understandable, Ghana's potential was not necessarily up to its intentions. In the case of cocoa processing, Ghana suffered from several handicaps – including distance from the main markets, unfavourable climate, inadequate supplies of water at a steady temperature, and lack of relevant skills -- which made large-scale processing of questionable viability. Nevertheless Ghana allowed itself to be persuaded by interests anxious to supply processing plant and machinery that viability could be assured. Two new processing plants were established, one at Tema and the other at Takoradi, at a price of £2.2m. each, with an 80 percent credit repayable at 4 percent over 4 years.[8] Plans for the Tema factory were extended in 1963, before any work on the original proposal had started, to four times its original capacity and almost four times its original cost. The new proposal, which was made on Nkrumah's orders and probably inspired by Drivici, was to include an entire complex capable of processing 200,000 tons a year into cocoa butter, powder, powder-products, and chocolate, plus a factory for milk powder and four giant storage silos with a capacity each of 50,000 tons. By the coup in 1966 only the cocoa silos and the chocolate factory had been built, but Ghana had paid 50 percent of the contract price (in down payment and debt-service), more than the cost of the work carried out by that date. Moreover, because of major design faults, the silos were useless for storing cocoa, and the chocolate factory could operate only at a heavy loss, serving only the minute domestic market. The behaviour of the contractors had been evasive throughout; they persistently refused to give any specifications of plant or equipment, to allow inspection of machinery, or even to supply the manufacturer's name before completion, on which the consultants retained by the Ministry of Industries had insisted. Work on the main project was therefore held up, but unfortunately not on the cocoa silos which still stand, fully paid and useless.

The main snag in the French-financed project was more straightforward. Again Ghana had been trapped into believing that it could reduce its import bill simply and quickly by constructing an integrated textile mill. The French suppliers offered Ghana what they called ultra-modern machinery, eventually supplying 500 looms (20,000 spindle capacity) out of a single batch of 1000 whose production in France was discontinued when mechanical defects were discovered. Ghana was, therefore, saddled with expensive but faulty machinery costing £3.5m., which made for constant snags in production, and required expatriate management – at a price – to keep it in operation, even at below half capacity.

The British-built steel mill, for an initial cost of £1.65m., and credit of £1.48m. to be repaid at 5½ percent over six years, was constructed and started operations on schedule. Planned capacity was for 30,000 tons per year, utilising some 40,000 tons of scrap, half of which seemed assured locally, as Ghana had already managed to export that quantity in the late 1950s. Basing the industry on scrap might possibly have made it commercially viable; but unless it started utilising Ghanaian ore its contribution to the economy was likely to remain very small. While competing contractors stressed the latter aspect, the only issue in doubt was who would get the contract, and this appears to have been settled without any objective appraisal. Ghana got a mill which was not capable, without additional expense, of handling the planned throughput of scrap. The builders accepted a management contract at a fixed fee, independent of performance (a common practice in Ghana), which also allowed them to incur any additional expenses required to bring facilities up to planned capacity; but they failed to make the necessary improvements before their contract was cancelled by the NLC.

The Czech shoe factory was beset by a whole host of problems. The initial idea came from the wish to substitute domestic production for a rapidly rising import (shoe imports had doubled between 1954 and 1960). The Czechs, as the main exporters to Ghana, were asked in 1961 to help with local production, and the shoe factory was eventually conceived as part of a grand design under which hides from cattle processed in the Bolgatanga meat factory would supply a Czech tannery, which in turn would provide the main input for the shoe factory at Kumasi for which the Czechs were to supply the equipment and training. When the shoe factory eventually came into production in 1967, the earlier phases of the production chain had gone badly wrong, so that it was left to depend indefinitely on imported leather. The shoe factory itself, even on this basis, had been assessed by the Czechs as capable of showing a profit, with an estimated rate of return of 10 percent on capital invested. But Western consultants considered the initial capital outlay as at least 50 percent too large for this to be realised; the factory plans included costly provisions for workshops, an office block, recreation facilities, canteens, etc. – none of which were essential – and which the Czechs insisted on as part of a 'new deal for labour', but which they themselves were not financing. In the end these trimmings virtually sabotaged the entire operation. The construction contract for the entire complex had been given to a British company; it, however, had to withdraw while work was in progress because it could not raise the required credit in Britain. This and other delays allowed six years to elapse between the original agreement with the Czechs (in 1961) and eventual production. In the meantime, both shoe-making technology and shoe styles had changed, so that the factory's output had become outdated. To add to the difficulties, three private shoe-making factories came into production at about the same time, producing cheaper and more fashionable shoes, leaving the state factory with its first six-months' output unsold.

Yugoslave credits (£0.5m. for 8 years at 3 percent interest) were made available for three canning factories, for pineapples at Nsawam, mango and tomato at Wenchi, and tomato at Pwalugu. The Yugoslavs, who were brought into this operation on Nkrumah's insistence, claimed that the three factories would be capable of a rate of return of between 15 percent and 20 percent. This calculation was based on the assumption of adequate raw material supplies and a ready market in Ghana or 'adjacent territories'; but no feasibility studies or market research had been done to test these assumptions. In fact, later estimates showed that available supplies of raw fruit were only enough for an output of a fraction of that which was planned: 10 percent for pineapples, 15 percent for tomatoes, and 50 percent for mangoes. Moreover, the bulk of demand at the planned rate of output would have had to come from outside Ghana: 60 percent for tomatoes, and almost 100 percent for pineapple (which were of a 'standard' grade and unsaleable at a price which was economic). As for mangoes, the planned output at Wenchi was more than double that coming annually into world trade.

Notes

1. Restated in Nkrumah's Speech in the National Assembly introducing the Seven-Year Plan, 11 March 1964.

2. *A Study of Contemporary Ghana* ed. by W. Birmingham, I. Neustadt and E.N. Omaboe, Allen and Unwin, 1966, pp.288--93.
3. Seven-Year Plan, p.19.
4. State Bakery, Boatyards, Brick and Tile, Cannery, Distillery, Furniture and Joinery, Match, Vegetable Oils, Metal Products, Sheet Metal, Timber Products, Tyre-Service, Hotels, Laundries, and Films.
5. Those completed produced aluminium cutlery, cement, cocoa products, fibre bags, glassware and bottles, paper cartons and containers, radio and television sets, steel angles and bars, steel drums, and sugar. Industries under construction were intended to produce asbestos cement, canned fruit and vegetables, cement, light bulbs, meat products, pencils and pens, pharmaceuticals, refined gold, shoes, sugar, tanned leather, textiles, tinned fish and fish meal, and tyres and tubes.
6. Nederlandse Creditverzeking Maatschappij, N.V.
7. Compagnie Franâise d'Assurance pour le Commerce Extérieur.
8. The Takoradi plant started operations in 1964, and despite early losses due to the artificially high price for raw cocoa which it had to pay, it at least demonstrated that some processes, on a modest scale, could be made viable.

Chapter 5 The Nkrumah Legacy

1. Ghana's public finances, balance of payments and economy at the time of the coup

In the months before Nkrumah was deposed in February 1966, almost exactly fifteen years after assuming office, Ghana's economy was in disarray. The statistics showed massive budget and balance of payments deficits – which could no longer be covered by orthodox means – exhausted foreign reserves, and a dangerously rising debt burden. For the average Ghanaian the country's economic difficulties made themselves felt through rising prices, growing shortages of goods, declining real incomes, reduced job opportunities, and heavier taxation. By 1966, while Ghana was technically not bankrupt, in the sense that it could in theory meet all its foreign obligations out of its own assets and earnings or new borrowing, in practice it was, since the government lacked the will or capacity to do so; and there seemed no prospect of it being able to do so for at least several years. The aim of this short chapter is to distinguish the immediate economic difficulties at the time of the coup from the underlying economic condition. This should provide a measure of the debt burden left as a legacy from Nkrumah, and show the extent to which the debt problem complicated rehabilitation policies after Nkrumah's down-fall.

During the last two years of Nkrumah's rule (1964 and 1965) – which were also the first two years of the Seven-Year Plan – Central Government spending on current account had reached £165m. and £181m. respectively; in 1959 and 1960 (the first two years of the Five-Year Plan) it had averaged £90m., which was already very large by earlier standards. Although revenue had grown rapidly too – largely as a result of increasing tax burdens – from £72m. in 1959–60 to £123m. in 1964 and £142m. in 1965, the growth rate was not fast enough; as a result the budget deficit increased from £18m. in 1959–60 to £42m. in 1964 and £39m. in 1965. The deficit in 1965 was the seventh annual deficit in succession. Since mid–1964, moreover, it had to be financed partly from short-term foreign borrowing and partly from Central Bank borrowing. This infusion of cash into the economy forced up internal demand and retail prices, which rose by almost 70 percent between

1963 and the coup. Production, however, lagged behind demand both in 1964 and even more notably in 1965, despite a very high level of public investment, which had risen from £35m. in 1959–60 to £87m. in 1964 and £101m. in 1965. Much of the investment had gone into non-productive or social projects (especially public buildings and education) and into long-maturing projects (e.g. the Volta scheme); and of that which had gone into state enterprises in agriculture and industry very little had as yet become operational. At the same time, private investment, especially in smaller businesses, had declined sharply from £52m. in 1959–60 to just over £30m. in both 1964 and 1965, as a result of uncertainties created by the expansion of state industries, the chaotic administration of the import licencing system, inflation which made speculative stock holding or house building more attractive, and excess capacity created by shortages of materials and spare parts. Output generally had been affected by input shortages due to foreign exchange scarcity. This scarcity continued despite tight import controls and high import duties and taxes on consumer goods, which had held the rise in imports between 1959–60 and 1964 to only £4m. (from £137m. to £141m.). In 1964 as much as 44 percent of the import bill was accounted for by food and 'maintenance imports' (fuels, raw materials, components, etc.); but even so there were continuing and severe shortages in both. In 1965 imports rose sharply, to £188m., with maintenance imports alone up by £10m.; but this was still not enough to satisfy demand, while chaos in the licencing system meant that imports were not spread among claimants according to a proper assessment of priorities. In fact, the share of food and maintenance imports in the total fell back to 37 percent as a result of big (non-food) consumer goods credit purchases from East Europe. These were made partly to appease growing public discontent and to stock shops in Accra in time for the OAU summit conference; but because of local sales resistance to these goods, which were considered inferior, they added to Ghana's short-term debts without adequately satisfying local consumer demand. The 1965 upsurge in imports was not matched by a corresponding rise in exports; in fact these had risen by only £5m. since 1959–60, from £121m. to £126m. – an indifferent performance partly accounted for by a disastrous slump in cocoa prices, which allowed Ghana to earn little more in 1965 than in 1959–60 despite a 40 percent increase in quantity exported. The overall adverse balance on current account, already £22m. in 1959–60, thus swung further into the red in 1965, to £80m.; this was also Ghana's seventh consecutive balance of payments deficit on current account. During 1964 and 1965, moreover, at least £25m. of the deficit was 'covered' by short-term borrowing (other than 180-day import credits) and unilaterally deferred payments.

The rapidly accumulating short-term debt, used to finance imports, including consumer imports, presented the most immediate problem for 1966. In that year around £40m., including arrears from 1965, was due (even without further borrowing). This was equivalent to 31 percent of Ghana's exports in 1965, or 36 percent of its projected exports in 1966, a financial burden large by any standard. (The figures exclude at least £15m. of accumulated arrears on private profit and dividend remittances and other miscellaneous payments which were, for the time being, frozen.) In addition to the short-term debt, £19m. in medium-term debt and another £1.5m. in long-term debt were due in 1966, giving a total debt obligation for the year of £60m., with the total debt equivalent to 49 percent of exports in 1965 and 55 percent of actual exports in 1966. The position for 1967 was a little better, but not much, with £31m. of medium- and long-term debt service payments falling due, and an estimated debt-ratio[1] of between 26 percent and 28 percent (assuming that Ghana could get by without incurring any debts during either 1966 or 1967, which was unlikely).

The total outstanding debt at the beginning of 1966, taking both capital and interest into account, came to at least £255m., made up of £15m. in miscellaneous arrears, £25m. in new short-term obligations, £155m. in medium-term (two to twelve years) credits on which goods and services had been delivered or were in the pipeline and £60m. in long-term loans, mainly for the Volta Project (plus arrears on remittances etc). Of the total of £255m., £163m., or 64 percent, was due in the five years 1966–70. The average external debt burden was thus scheduled at £33m. a year (or £24.6m. on medium- and long-term debt) giving an average annual debt burden of between 20 percent and 30 percent of exports depending on the exact export performance over the five years, and again assuming that Ghana incurred no new debts from the beginning of 1966.

Ghana was thus incapable of taking on any new servicing commitments for the next five years. It was clear that to continue with the rates of spending and importing reached in 1964 or 1965 was foolish. Even the lower rates achieved in 1963 (public spending of £130m. and imports of £140m.) would have required further credits of not less than about £50m. An additional debt burden of this magnitude, to allow Ghana to continue its pre-1966 policies for just another year, would therefore have raised annual debt payments for 1966–70 to over

£40m., to give a debt-ratio of somewhere between 25 percent and 35 percent; this would have been unmanageable even if the export and domestic output performances of 1963–5 had been revived as a result of continued high public spending.

But it is unlikely, in any case, that Ghana would have been allowed to accumulate this amount of additional debt. Already in 1965 a number of Western governments, including the British, had imposed severe restrictions on medium-term credit insurance to Ghana; while not drying up the flow entirely, they had reduced it and, more important still, the number of sources from which credits in large numbers were previously obtained. Moreover, by early 1966 some suppliers were unwilling to fill further orders because payments were in arrears, or because they did not wish to extend credit, or were unable to obtain easy or sufficiently cheap insurance on export credits. So, even if Nkrumah had not been deposed in February, Ghana would have had to cut back drastically on its spending plans sometime during 1966, either on its own initiative, or through exhausted credit. Even default provided no easy way out, since what Ghana would have saved on its debt payments would not have sufficed to maintain the flow of imports at the 1965, or even the 1963, level.

Coup or no coup, Ghana had thus finally come to the last stretch of the particular road it had followed since the mid-1950s; it faced an extremely difficult task of readjustment in the years immediately ahead. But had it made some lasting gains in the meantime? And how well prepared was it to advance again once its immediate financial, external payments, and economic problems could be sorted out?

2. Major changes in Ghana's economy between 1950–53 and 1962–5

i) Employment and the supply of skills

Between 1950–53 and 1962–5 Ghana's population increased from about 5.3m. to 7.4m., or at a rate of 3 percent a year. The active labour force stayed at 40 percent of the population throughout. Over the period there were, however, considerable shifts in employment as between different sectors: the share of those engaged in agriculture (other than cocoa), forestry, and fishing remained constant at 41 percent; the share of two other traditional sectors, cocoa and mining, declined from 22 percent to 16 percent and 4 percent to 2 percent respectively; while the shares of industry rose from 7 percent to 8 percent, of construction from 3 percent to 4 percent and of services (including public administration, commerce, transport, and personal services) from 23 percent to 29 percent. Of the total labour force, only a minority was in paid employment, the rest being employers or self-employed (about 70 percent), family workers, share-croppers, and apprentices. The actual number of paid employees rose from 325,000 in 1950–53 (or 15 percent of the labour force) to 510,000 in 1962–65 (or 17 percent of the labour force).

The most spectacular single change in employment was the expansion in public employment, from 98,000 in 1950–53 to 252,000 in 1962–5, or from one-third to almost one-half of all paid employment. Large numbers of those employed in the public sector, particularly after 1961, filled what were virtually sinecure jobs in the administration, in the state farms and state corporations; the jobs having been either created to soak up unemployment or left filled even when they ceased to serve any useful purpose.

Labour productivity among many of those employed in the rural areas, particularly in petty trading, remained low, but actual unemployment was rare; indeed the acute shortage of seasonal labour attracted an increasing flow of immigrants from neighbouring countries, accounting for as much as 40 percent of the hired help in cocoa farming in the sixties. In the urban areas, in contrast, unemployment was high throughout. The 1960 census listed 165,000 as unemployed and looking for work; this was 20 percent of the urban work force. No accurate figures for the earlier period are available, but it is clear that the urban work force increased more rapidly than the number of jobs throughout the 'fifties. After 1960 urban unemployment increased, if anything more quickly than before, despite government efforts to soak up the rising demand for paid jobs through the public sector. Given the fact that there was no open unemployment in the urban areas, the phenomenon of rising urban unemployment was only partly the result of the overall increase in population; in part it reflected also the rapid rate of increase in migration from country to town (the latter accounting for 27 percent of the total population in 1965 compared to 15 percent in 1950), and the rapid expansion in the primary school system.

Major changes occurred in this period in education and in the skill endowment of the population. Primary and middle-school enrolment increased from 20 percent to about 70 percent of the relevant age groups between 1950 and 1965. Numbers in secondary schools shot up more than ten-fold, from 3,500 to 42,000; and in teacher training institutions and universities from 2,000 to 14,000 and from 200 to

4,000 respectively.

In the lower and middle skill ranges numbers in apprenticeships or in vocational courses provide a better index of change than members enrolled in ordinary schools. The number of apprentices appears to have grown little in the period (there were 40,000 recorded in the 1960 Census), but formal vocational enrolment rose from under 1,000 in 1950–53 to almost 5,000 in 1965. Moreover, the establishment of a number of large private industrial enterprises and state enterprises (including the state farms with their repair shops, the Fishing Corporation, the airways and shipping lines, the Volta River Authority and the manufacturing enterprises) vastly expanded the number of Ghanaians receiving some form of on-the-job craft, technical, or clerical training. Nevertheless, while the number of clerical workers, skilled craftsmen, technicians, and skilled production workers had increased by several hundred thousands, their supply was still far short of what Ghana needed in the middle sixties. At the higher levels of skill, there is a more direct relationship between the expansion of education and the supply of skills, or at least the raw material for administrative, managerial, or professional posts; numbers may therefore be assumed to have risen quickly through the very rapid expansion in higher education in Ghana and in the numbers of Ghanaians receiving training abroad. Between 1950 and 1960, the general administrative staff of the Civil Service was almost entirely Africanised. This was a considerable achievement, although the replacement of departing British Colonial Service Officers by Ghanaians did not increase the numbers of skilled officers; overall, general standards declined, especially after 1960, with the recruitment of undertrained or inexperienced officers and the proliferation of political appointments, particularly in the public corporations and state enterprises. Moreover, the shortage of recruits with technical skills, such as in engineering, geology, veterinary medicine, agriculture, and forestry, already severe in 1950, was still more acute in 1965; many posts, particularly in agriculture, remained vacant, and the expansion in education, health, and the public services had relied heavily on expatriates. At the time of the 1966 coup, there were in all about 35,000 Ghanaians with 'high level' skills, their numbers having more than quadrupled since 1950; there were also some 4,000 expatriates, including some 2,500 working within the public sector, of which some 1,000 were in teaching or in advisory or executive posts paid for out of technical assistance funds. In all, the number of expatriates had increased since 1950, although many of the newcomers, in contrast to their predecessors, stayed for relatively short periods, which tended to reduce their effective contribution.

ii) Trends in domestic income and expenditure

Ghana's GDP, recorded at ruling market prices, increased two-and-a-half times between 1950–53 and 1962–5 (see Appendix, Table A2). Measured in constant prices the increase was, however, only twofold. Given the 3 percent annual increase in population GDP *per capita* increased by only a third over the period, from an average of £55 in 1950–53 to £73 in 1962–5, both measured in 1960 prices. On the basis of figures published by the World Bank, Ghana's growth rate was somewhat slower than the average for developing Africa as a whole, but faster than that of several countries with similar or larger populations, such as Cameroon, Malawi, and Zaire, and considerably faster than, for example, that of Egypt or Morocco. In the first half of the sixties, Ghana grew slower than most, but this period followed ten years when Ghana was among the leaders. The record of the 'fifties looks good also in a historical perspective; between 1910 and 1960 Ghana's real GDP per caput is estimated to have doubled, with two-fifths of this improvement accounted for by the last decade before 1960.

The usual measure of changing living standards is the rate of change in real consumption per caput. Between 1950–53 and 1958–61 consumption grew more quickly than GDP (by 0.5 percent a year), but in 1962–5, although GDP showed a small rise, consumption declined sharply, by an average of over 3 percent a year. The periods of fastest growth in consumption (1954–7 and 1958–61) were also those of rising investment, and this was made possible by an excess of imports over exports (averaging £6m. and £22m. a year respectively) financed largely by the run-down of reserves. In 1962–5, exports exceeded imports by an average of £3m. a year (when measured in constant 1960 prices); the trade surplus and the continued high investment could only be maintained at the expense of consumption.

The external surplus for 1962–5 referred to above needs further comment. In this period there was in fact a large external trade deficit measured at current prices (see Table A 10), which was offset by the run-down of reserves and by foreign borrowing. However, if trade flows are revalued at constant 1960 prices, the period shows a small surplus. The difference between the current price and constant price figures gives an indication of the extent to which Ghana was affected by the worsening of its terms of trade during 1962–5, as compared with earlier years. Moreover, they give an indication, too, of the additional effort required from Ghana, in relative terms, to maintain a given real level of GDP, consumption and investment.

The ratio of investment to GDP is sometimes used as an index of development 'effort', and the domestic savings ratio as an index of 'self-help' or success in mobilising domestic resources for development. On the first, Ghana's record shows up very well, rising from 13 percent in 1950–53 to 20 percent in 1962–5; few developing countries have recorded such a rapid increase or a level of investment even approaching 20 percent of GDP. The crude investment ratio, however, is at best an imperfect index, with an implicit assumption about the 'quality' of investment. Ghana provides a perfect example of its ambiguity: here increasing investment was accompanied first by an acceleration, and then by a progressive slowing down, in the growth rate of GDP. Ghana's savings performance was good in 1950–53 and again in 1962–5, with 20.0 percent and 20.5 percent of GDP respectively; in the intervening period of rapidly growing public and private consumption the rate was down to 14.5 percent of GDP. The high rate of savings in the earliest period reflects low government recurrent spending and solid budget surpluses, as well as the big surpluses of the Cocoa Marketing Board which were invested overseas rather than within Ghana. The rate in 1962–5 reflects a very high level of public savings, through heavy taxation and a low producer price paid to cocoa farmers, as well as forced 'savings' through the deficit (inflationary) financing and import control policies of the government. The superficially solid savings performance in this period was spoiled, however, by the fact that not all the savings were put to constructive use.

iii) Changes in the sectoral distribution of income

One of the central aims of Nkrumah's policy was to achieve a restructuring of Ghana's economy, reducing its dependence on agriculture, including cocoa exports, and promoting the development of industry, particularly in the area of import substitutes. Between 1950–53 and 1962–5 some considerable changes did indeed take place in the sectoral origins of output and incomes, although it remains open to argument whether these changes strengthened or weakened the economy – or indeed the extent to which they reflect policy rather than spontaneous developments outside government control.

The actual changes in the income shares of the six main sectors of the economy are summarised in Table 5.1; for comparison the table also shows the changes in the distribution of employment between these sectors. The statistical basis for the table is not as firm as one would wish, and the figures should therefore be taken as no more than general indicators of the direction of change between the main sectors. Moreover, the figures do not show up a number of interesting changes within the main sectors themselves; but an indication of these is given in the text.

Ghana's strategic, but declining, dependence on all forms of agricultural incomes – from 54 percent to 46 percent of the total – stands out clearly. The output of food crops did no better than keep in line with the increase in the agricultural labour force, which had remained constant as a proportion of the total labour force despite the relative decline in the rural population. Patterns and techniques of cultivation remained virtually unchanged, and the increased output was made possible largely by utilising new land, which by 1965 was beginning to be in short supply in some areas; but the overall position was as yet far from critical. The unchanging modes of cultivation mirror the general isolation of peasant farmers from new ideas and their relative neglect by the government. In the few places where concentrated help was provided either by government or by private concerns, in the form of irrigation improvements or supervised use of fertiliser or marketing, there were some significant improvements in yields, though on a limited scale, and a few new crops were introduced to some areas, including rice, sugar, and tomatoes, and some non-food crops including cotton, tobacco, and rubber. The state farms, which had after 1960 absorbed the biggest slice of public funds for agriculture, had made little impact on output. Agricultural exports (other than cocoa) remained stagnant at round £1m. a year throughout the period. In 1950 Ghana had already been a food importer on a considerable scale; at that time this reflected the relatively high level of incomes and preference for imported (or prestige) foods, rather than any permanent overall shortage; but this was no longer the case in 1962–5.

Imports of food in 1950–53, at an annual average of £11m., were already an important factor in the balance of payments; they rose to £14m. in 1962–5, and although imports by then had fallen rapidly as a percentage of total food consumption, the drain on foreign exchange was by then relatively more serious. The most significant improvements in agriculture (outside cocoa farming) were in forestry and fishing, where output expanded very rapidly.

The increased shares of output and incomes from forestry and fishing marked an important relative shift within agriculture from lower to higher productivity and income activities. Growth in the former also helped to increase exports and provided wider opportunities for simple manufacturing, while in the latter it served to improve the average diet, allowed for some domestic substitution of a major food import, and some new opportunities for local processing. All these were solid and lasting gains. But the lack of major progress in food growing was the major failure of the Nkrumah regime, as indeed it had been of the colonial authorities before. In 1965 food output lagged behind demand more than ever before, and the average diet remained poor, with insufficient protein content. Moreover, much the same proportion of the labour force as in 1950–53 was engaged in food growing, but this took a lower share of income. As an occupation it offered even fewer rewards and scope for savings which could be ploughed back into farming or invested in other, expanding, sectors.

Table 5.1 Changes in the sectoral structure of incomes and employment between 1950–53 and 1962–65.

	Percentage share of GDP at 1960 factor cost		Percentage share of total employment	
	1950–53	1962–65	1950–53	1962–65
Agriculture	35.0	31.5	41.0	41.0
Cocoa	19.0	14.0	22.0	16.0
Mining	5.5	3.5	4.0	2.0
Industry	4.0	11.5	7.0	8.0
Construction	6.5	7.0	3.0	4.0
Services	30.0	33.0	23.0	29.0
Total GDP (£m)	280.0	500.0	–	–
Employment (000's)	–	–	2,150	3,000

Notes: See Appendix, Table A 3

Sources: See Statistical Appendix and table A 3.

Cocoa had had a chequered history in the sixteen years between 1950 and 1965. In the first place it recovered magnificently from the disease crisis of the late 1940s which had threatened its entire future. By means of vigorous campaigns to control swollen-shoot disease in the early 1950s – which led to large-scale replanting – and against capsids disease in the mid-and late 1950s, backed up by provision of new tree varieties more resistant to bad weather, output had increased from an annual average of 240,000 tons in 1950–53 to 460,000 in 1962–5, a gain of 90 percent. At the same time, due to poor export prices in the sixties, made worse by the inept handling of sales on Ghana's part after 1961, export earnings increased from £56m. to £72m., or a gain of only 30 percent. The increase in output, and the smaller increase in earning, had been achieved with much the same land area and much the same number of workers. Ghana's dependence on cocoa incomes was also reduced, but this happened in a way which certainly no one would have intended, i.e. through falling export prices. Despite heavy taxation on cocoa production, average annual earnings (after tax) for each person permanently engaged in cocoa cultivation did rise from £70 to £80. But inflation meant that the purchasing power of these earnings in 1962–5 was no more than £50, or nearly 30 percent less than in 1950–53.

By 1965 cocoa faced a new and serious crisis, in terms of both supply and demand. One of the root causes of the crisis, which affected the whole economic structure of the industry and therefore its ability to compete in world markets, went back to the major replanting in the early 1950s. At that time, a major opportunity had been lost to introduce both higher yielding tree varieties and newly developed methods of planting and cultivation (e.g. by using fertiliser); many of Ghana's competitors had made these improvements and Ghana now faced a rapid erosion of its formerly considerable cost advantage. Its techniques had changed little for several decades, continuing to rely on labour – and land-intensive methods, using little capital other than spraying equipment and few bought inputs other than pesticides. The use of the latter had spread rapidly in the fifties, but after the withdrawal of subsidies during the cocoa glut had again declined, with a consequent reduction in yields. With increasing money costs of labour and land, and increasing opportunity costs of land, cocoa cultivation was becoming relatively less profitable to the farmers and less remunerative to the economy. The most important way of counter-acting these trends was by economising on land, and on the labour required for land clearance – i.e. by measures aimed at increasing yields both per acre and per man; and this is precisely what Ghana was failing to do.

The performance of industry, on which Nkrumah had placed so much hope, looks impressive – having increased its share from 4 percent to 11.5 percent of GDP between 1950–53 and 1962–5; but it should be remembered that over the period mining, cocoa, and other agricultural incomes together rose only very slowly, which tended to exaggerate the relative performance of industry. Even so, in absolute terms the contribution of industry to income rose threefold during the period, and to employment by somewhat less.

Between 1950 and 1965 several thousand more small manufacturing establishments (employing up to five persons) came into being, producing a wide range of goods by essentially craft methods. There was little change in techniques since 1950 except that electricity was much more widely available; but the number and range of products from such small establishments increased rapidly, and the value of output by as much as 100 percent. In addition almost 200 manufacturing establishments employing 30--100 workers, and another 100 which were still larger, were set up; thirty-seven of these units were in the state sectors, nine more were part public, and the rest entirely private. While 'large-scale' industry in 1950 had been confined largely to public utilities, saw-milling or other wood processing, and workshops maintained by the mines, the railways, and road transport undertakings, by 1965 private or joint-enterprise industries produced a wide range of other goods -- at a commercial return -- including processed foods, tobacco products, soft drinks, beer and spirits, textiles and clothing, leather and rubber products, chemicals, petrol, soap, aluminium products, vehicles, radio and television sets. The state enterprises already in operation were commercially unsuccessful as a group, although a number of those started before 1962 did manage to show a profit. While the range of their output was quite extensive (see Ch. 4) the total value of their contribution to manufacturing was by 1965 still very small, at about £4m. gross value added, which was about half the contribution expected from the Volta scheme, with a comparable investment outlay.

A major drawback to Ghana's industrial development was import dependence, particularly of the larger enterprises. One of the prime motives behind the industrial drive, particularly after 1961, had been to save foreign exchange; but during 1962–5, the foreign exchange burden was, if anything, greater than the saving, even allowing for the foreign credits which financed 40 percent of the capital investment in state enterprises and the small net inflow of foreign capital. For a long period ahead, only small net savings in foreign exchange from industry could be expected, and even that only if the foreign debt payments and remittance of profits due over the next five years were excluded. In part, this is inevitable when industrial development implies total dependence initially on foreign know-how, patents, equipment, spare parts, and components. In Ghana's case this phase was likely to be particularly long. In addition, the country was entirely dependent, and would inevitably remain so, on imported fuels and lubricants, and the raw materials for many of the industries. Moreover, Ghana had embarked on industries in which the domestic value added was small in relation to the value of the components or processed materials which had to be imported; most notably the food processing, beverage, textile, leather, glass, cement, metal, and assembly industries. These industries were chosen partly because the production processes involved were straightforward; but at the same time they could make only a small net contribution in value added, new employment, or foreign exchange savings.

iv) The growth of the public sector

Another of the central tenets of Nkrumah policy was that the public sector should play a more prominent part in the economy. Until 1961 no diminution in the role of the private sector was implied; it was hoped, rather, to stimulate the private sector through more vigorous public policies. After 1961, following the CPP's formal commitment to a 'socialist' model of development, communal consumption in the form of improved services, such as health care or education, was given precedence over additional personal consumption; but even the major developments in state agriculture and industry were initially at least aimed at supplementing and encouraging, and not replacing, productive investment in the private sector.

Table 5.2 Changes in the importance of the public sector between 1950–53 and 1962–65.

(annual average, constant 1960 prices)

	1950 – 53 (£m.)	Share in GDP (%)	1962 – 65 (£m.)	Share in GDP (%)
Public consumption	20.5	7.0	67.2	12.4
Public investment	13.7	4.7	77.8	14.4
Total public spending	34.2	11.7	145.0	26.8
Public revenue	37.6	13.0	97.2	18.0
Balance	3.4	1.3	–47.8	-8.8

Notes and Sources: See Statistical Appendix and Table A 4.

Table 5.2 shows the rise in the importance of the public sector. Public consumption more than trebled in real terms, and its share of GDP nearly doubled; public investment went up almost six-fold, its share in GDP trebled, and the share of public investment in total investment doubled, from 36 percent to 72 percent. Contrary to intentions, the primary effect of this growth was to increase the relative size of the public sector at the expense of the private sector, adding only to a limited extent to the growth capacity of the private sector, and exposing the entire economy to a much greater direct dependence on public spending than ever before. Moreover, as can be seen from the figures for total public revenue, the economy had in 1962–5 become not only more dependent on public spending as such, but also on public spending which was financed to a large extent from internal (including Central Bank) and external borrowing.

The bulk of public spending, on both capital and recurrent accounts combined, went on infrastructure and public services, public buildings, and general administration (55 percent in 1950–53, declining to 50 percent in 1962–5); and education and health (31 percent in 1950–53, declining to 27 percent -- see Appendix, Table A 5). The government's plans for increasing the economic potential of the country, from which the private sector could benefit both in the short and long run, rested initially on major improvements in infrastructure and general public services. The improvements achieved during the 1950s were both impressive and necessary, although funds were also squandered in needlessly lavish projects, and spending plans did not take into account sufficiently priority economic needs. The railways had been extended and modernised; Takoradi harbour and a string of smaller fishing ports had been improved and a new harbour at Tema completed; the road network had been more than doubled; public transport, including air transport, and telephone and postal services had been extended; water supplies and public amenities improved, in both urban and rural areas; industrial sites laid out; government information and publication services extended; new employment exchanges opened; administrative improvements carried out, affecting among others the cocoa inspectorate, the customs and excise and inland revenue, and the statistical services. The record in the 1960s was, in contrast, unsatisfactory. A number of useful improvements were made, with the completion of the Akosombo dam and hydro-electric project as a notable example, but resources were also squandered in low priority or lavish public works projects, examples of which have already been given (see Ch. 4, Section 4). Moreover, while funds were being spent freely on new projects and new construction work, maintenance of existing facilities was badly neglected. Thus, the railway system had fallen into a state of disrepair, as had many roads, including many of those built in the 1950s; whole fleets of buses and lorries were out of commission through poor maintenance or lack of spare parts; this was also the case with other equipment, from dock cranes or cocoa weighing machines to office equipment. Also, public facilities had frequently been expanded beyond a level at which they could be serviced or staffed by the then available supply of skilled personnel. By 1965 Ghana's infrastructure and public services, while further expanded, were in a worse state than five years earlier, with a sizeable share of the new plant or new facilities remaining under-used.

Although the growth in public revenue could not keep pace with the exceptionally fast growth of public spending, the increase both in absolute terms and as a share of GDP was impressive. The net burden of Central Government taxes alone rose from 13 percent to 15 percent of GDP (at factor cost). Over the period from 1950–53 to 1962–5 there were also major changes in the structure of Central Government revenue and taxation (see Appendix, Table A 7). Most significantly, the share of cocoa duties (and levies) in total revenue declined from 45 percent to only 16 percent (rising in money terms from an annual average of £15m. to £17.5m.) Their place was taken largely by increased excise and import duties and purchase taxes, whose combined share rose from 29 percent to 51 percent of total revenue (with the share of import duties alone up from 27 percent to 36 percent). While the reduced dependence on cocoa could be welcomed, the new dependence on import taxes, particularly at a time when foreign exchange shortages allowed little room for expanding consumer goods imports, brought its own dangers.

v) The balance of payments

Another important aim of Nkrumah's policy had been to reduce Ghana's overall dependence on foreign trade, particularly on the export of raw cocoa. In the event, the share of exports in GDP (both measured in constant 1960 prices) declined from 30 percent to 29 percent, and the share of imports increased from 23 percent to 28 percent (see Appendix, Table A 9). The corresponding shares measured in current prices, however, both declined, from 33 percent to 18 percent and from 27 percent to 23 percent respectively, turning a healthy surplus on goods and services into a substantial deficit. The performance of exports was disappointing, although the fault was not all Ghana's: their value increased by only 50 percent between 1950–53 and 1962–5 whereas their volume doubled. But Ghana had also done little to diversify its exports. Only 10 percent of the value of cocoa exports in 1962–5 was in processed form. The share of six traditional exports had declined from 96 percent to 89 percent of the total, but this was due largely to stagnation in total cocoa proceeds. By the end of the 1960s aluminium exports from the Kaiser smelter would provide a useful new source of foreign earnings, but no other important developments were in sight. Ghana's export earnings therefore remained exposed to the vagaries of the world cocoa market.

The structure of imports, in contrast to that of exports, changed very considerably. Consumer goods (including food) fell from 56 percent to 39 percent of all imports; 'intermediate goods' (including building materials) and capital equipment, on the other hand, both rose quickly, increasing their shares from 32 percent to 36 percent and 12 percent to 25 percent respectively. In addition the bill for imported services – insurance, transport etc. – quintupled from under £4m. to £20m. The relatively slow growth in consumer imports reflects artificial restraints imposed since 1961 rather than any slowing down in demand. The rapid rise in imports of intermediate goods reflects the growth of industry based on imported raw materials, components, etc. as well as the high import component in construction. Thus while Ghana had managed to engineer at least a temporary reduction in its dependence on imports for final consumer goods, domestic output had itself been made more dependent on imports. And already in 1964 and 1965 domestic output was severely hampered by the shortage of necessary imports resulting from the general scarcity in foreign exchange and the maladministration of the import licencing system.

Ghana's overall balance of payments current account position had changed from an annual average surplus of £14.0m. in 1950–53 to an annual average deficit of £46.5m. – of which £30.7m. represented the deficit on goods and services, and the remaining £15.8m. net factor incomes, debt service payments, and private recorded transfers overseas (see Appendix, Table A 10). With debt-servicing commitments already entered into by the end of 1965 amounting to £33m. on average over the next five years, the annual current account deficit during 1966–70 – other things remaining unchanged – would have increased to almost £75m.

3. The hard-core problems left from the Nkrumah era

It is now possible to summarise the hard-core problems which were bequeathed by the Nkrumah government to its successors.

The first, and single most important, problem was the economy's much increased dependence on public spending, in particular deficit spending. Economic activity outside agriculture was after 1950–53 largely sustained by the rapid growth in such spending. Investment spending stimulated a large and expanding building and construction sector, and a wide range of ancillary manufacturing, craft, transport and service enterprises. Public spending in general, on wages and local products, maintained a high level of demand, which encouraged the supply of simple locally-produced goods and of services, particularly in transport, commerce, and personal services. In fact, a whole pyramid of activity was founded on the demand created by public spending, with its viability dependent on the continued injection of purchasing power into the economy through the public sector. Employment was similarly linked, both directly and indirectly, to an expanding public sector, with an ever greater danger of mass 'open' unemployment (following a contraction in the public sector), owing to rapid urbanisation and growth in formal primary education. The political implications of a contraction in the public sector also grew progressively more dangerous – both from the point of view of the likely reaction to loss of livelihoods, and from the psychological impact of recession on a population conditioned to expansion (even if only of money incomes) by the end of the Nkrumah era.

The second problem was Ghana's increased dependence on imports for maintaining its own output. The increasing import content of production, resulting from the greater overall importance of industry and from the type of industries which were set up, in the public sector especially, and the simultaneous failure to develop new exports required utmost economy in imports of final consumer goods. The relative scope for such economies had already been much reduced by 1965. Moreover, reductions already achieved, and *a fortiori* further reductions, required Ghana to maintain a system of controls or import management for which its administrative capacity was as yet inadequate. A related problem was the increased dependence of government revenues on imports; slow growth in consumer imports thus limited the growth in public revenue or, alternatively, the imposition of compensatory duties on intermediate imports was liable to discourage investment and output.

The third problem was the failure to give proper encouragement to the peasant farmer in general and to encourage food cultivation in particular; this was a problem which Nkrumah himself inherited from the colonial period. In one sense, the neglect of agriculture was the mirror of the first two problems mentioned. The problem may also be seen from another angle. Despite unchanging techniques of food growing, output had expanded with the labour force because land was still in adequate supply; but with a growth rate in population of over 3 percent a year Ghana could not rely on this 'solution' indefinitely. Rising land prices, shorter periods of fallow, and the increasing encroachment of food cultivation on the main cocoa-growing areas were all pointers to land scarcity. After the long period of neglect, including underprovision of rural infrastructure, services and general amenities, the revitalisation of the countryside and modernisation of food growing techniques were bound to be both slow and difficult.

The fourth main problem was that posed by Ghana's state enterprises. At the time of the coup, the state farms were essentially still in their acclimatisation stage, and the enormous industrial programme launched since 1961 was still far from complete; only thirteen factories had started up, nineteen more were under construction, and work on some others was on the point of being started. In early 1966 the real worth of most of these enterprises – and of the infrastructure projects under construction – was uncertain. Some obviously never could be viable, such as the Yugoslav-financed canneries, or the Drivici food processing complex; others were, or could easily be made, viable, such as the Philips television and radio assembly plant, or some of the state farms. Because of the employment these enterprises did or could provide, and because such large investments had been sunk into them, there was a strong temptation, in those cases where there was just a chance that they might be made viable, to give them the benefit of the doubt and try to keep them in being. There was thus the serious danger that money, scarce administrative and managerial talent and foreign exchange would be used on enterprises, which would remain indefinitely burdens on the economy, or whose return could not justify additional outlays.

Finally, there was the complex of problems created by Ghana's increased dependence on foreign equipment, supplies and skills, and most important in the next five years, on foreign creditors. Many of the policies which Nkrumah had instigated, and which had in part at least been prompted by the desire to make the country less dependent on world markets and on Western industrial countries, had helped to consolidate that very dependence. And, because of the foreign debt Ghana had amassed, and the size of its debt obligations in relation to its likely foreign earnings over the five years 1966–70 in particular, it had to consider in all it did the likely reaction of its creditors. Thus while the task of overcoming the four main problems listed above was ultimately Ghana's responsibility and could be carried some way forward independently of its creditors' actions, the latter now had the power to simplify or to complicate the rehabilitation effort, through their response to any request for debt relief or to default on Ghana's part. At the same time, the way was also open to Ghana to use to its own advantage the special bargaining power – even though it was small – that the debt gave it. Both the creditors and their governments (through the guarantees they had given) had some interest in an orderly settlement of the debt and in preventing wholesale default, if only because this could set a precedent to be followed by other, more important, debtor countries.

Note

1. Debt-ratio - payments of principal, interest, and service charges on all foreign debts of one year or more, as a proportion of total foreign earnings.

Chapter 6 Post-Nkrumah Efforts at Rehabilitation and Debt Settlement

1. The programme of stabilisation under the NLC

There were three main tasks in the economic field facing the National Liberation Council (NLC) which was formed after Nkrumah was deposed. First, it had to come to terms with creditors on the arrears and debt-service payments due in the remaining ten months of 1966. Second, and affected by the outcome of the first, it had to curtail the import bill for the year to the foreign exchange that was likely to be available, and at the same time ensure that Ghana could continue to import essential supplies from reputable sources on normal commercial terms. Third, it had to review the government's tax and spending programmes to prevent complete collapse in the finances of the public sector, and at the same time reduce demand for imports with the minimum possible dislocation of domestic output.

Urgent as these tasks were, it should be remembered that the NLC had other cares which required immediate attention. It had to consolidate its position, deal with dissidents, and ensure the loyalty of the Civil Service. While the wish to restore financial and payments order was an important reason behind the coup, to which detailed attention was given once full authority was established, there were other objectives which the organisers of the coup also wished to promote. These included restoration of good relations with Western, and neighbouring African, countries; efficient and honest government; a return to a democratic form of government and the rule of law; a return to fewer economic controls and renewed emphasis on free private enterprise. All these objectives had important consequences for Ghana's future economic prospects, although they had their own, independent, rationale. Their pursuit had an important bearing on Ghana's relations with its main creditors, both in the NLC's period and in the two years under the Busia administration.

When the NLC came to power it at once turned for help to the IMF and to those Western governments which Nkrumah had spent a great deal of his later years in denouncing. This initiative was as unsurprising politically as it was necessary financially. The NLC was clearly oriented towards the West, and was anxious to re-establish friendlier relations with the governments of those countries. Moreover, it was reasonable for the NLC to expect some favours in return, especially if the rapprochement could be underlined by a strong domestic assault on all those actions of the former regime most repugnant to the West; in this category belonged not only Nkrumah's courting of the East and the accompanying sniping at the West, but also his authoritarianism and coercion at home. In practical terms, the exigencies of the financial situation required the goodwill of the West: by far the bulk of Ghana's outstanding external loans and commercial debt was owed to Western companies; its export markets were almost entirely in the West; and the greater part of its imports came from there. The NLC came to the conclusion that a political realignment with the West on international issues, and a renunciation of Nkrumah at home, were not enough; such gestures had to be accompanied by a more practical demonstration of good faith. The most practical expression was prompt and correct action on the international debt. This was the NLC's most important single decision. It not only determined the rules within which economic management was to be conducted and Ghana's future relations with the international financial community, but also saddled Ghana with the full consequences of Nkrumah's mistakes in the management of credit policy and of the abuses and inefficiency of foreign suppliers. In declaring its unreserved intention of honouring all its debts the NLC won a valuable (if temporary) respite and some admiration in international business circles; but it also threw away what had been, in effect, one of its few valuable cards for future debt and aid negotiations (see below, Section 3).

Having won the backing of the IMF, and obtained an agreed moratorium on further debt payments and thereby also secured a continued supply of imports, the NLC used the breathing space to tackle the balance of payments and budgetary problems. The first priority was to re-establish equilibrium by making economies where possible. In the preparation of remedial policies, the NLC followed the advice of the IMF, both because this was required in return for a stand-by credit, and because the NLC was generally convinced – in contrast to Nkrumah's suspicions – of the soundness of the advice to be obtained from that quarter. Nkrumah had found earlier IMF suggestions unpalatable, although in September 1965 he had agreed to try the emergency policies the IMF then advocated; the NLC was ready – even enthusiastic – to accept its counsels from the start. The receptiveness to orthodox Western advice in general became part and parcel of Ghana's new style of government.

The initial aims of the stabilisation programme were the reduction, (and eventually the elimination) of Central Bank financing of budget deficits, and the cutting back of the payments' deficits on current account to a level at which they would be balanced by inflows of long-term capital. Although the NLC placed the main emphasis on stringent economies – cutting the coat to the available cloth – it was to its credit that during the difficult early period it did not neglect entirely more positive measures aimed at stimulating exports, domestic output, and public revenue.

The stabilisation programme consisted essentially of four measures: (1) a squeeze on public spending; (2) a 'shake-out' of labour from the public sector; (3) tariff, duty, and import licence changes; and (4) devaluation. Each of these had a short- and long-term budgetary and balance of payments rationale. The overall impact was sharply deflationary, with both economic and political consequences.

The main deflationary element in the programme was the squeeze on public expenditure, achieved largely by stringent economies in public employment and a temporary halt on new public investment. While a revised budget was being prepared, the NLC tried to keep spending on recurrent account strictly to the estimates in the last (Nkrumah) budget (which the former regime had not managed to do for years), and this target was later cut down by another 2.5 percent. In the first NLC budget, presented in July 1966, recurrent spending was further cut by the introduction of modest school charges (thus breaking the sacrosanct Nkrumah principle of completely free public schooling) and by limitations on new public employment. In addition, a stringent policy of cutting out surplus staff in the Civil Service, the Public Corporations and the Workers Brigade was initiated, with rapid results. The NLC announced that it had 'started the process of systematically laying-off workers who are not contributing anything to production', adding in an ironic note that there was no 'intention that these workers who were previously being paid for doing nothing should continue to do nothing, the only difference this time being that the Government (would) not pay them.'[1] A substantial saving was achieved by cut-backs in civilian public employment; this was a politically courageous act and had much to commend it in economic terms.

In the first post-Nkrumah year the rise in Central Government recurrent expenditure was contained; it actually fell by £8m. from its 1965 level of £110m. However, by the end of 1967 it was already above the 1965 level and in 1968 it reached £148m. The initial savings from the cut-back in public employment were soon offset by the 5 percent increase in public service remunerations granted in July 1967. While it is true that real wages in the public sector had been falling since 1962, and that there was a long-term need to offer salaries which would attract suitable recruits, the timing of the increase may be questioned. The Mills-Odoi Commission[2] recommended very strongly against any further increases for some time, on the grounds that the economy could ill afford them. The higher salaries, the price rises after a 30 percent devaluation in mid-1967, and the increase in debt-service charges all made the rise in recurrent spending more or less inevitable.

It is interesting to note that force of circumstances made it as difficult for the NLC to keep down recurrent spending as it had been for Nkrumah, despite the former's earnest wish to do so. Not only did unforeseen claims arise, as in the old days, but sound arguments could always be produced why an increase should be allowed somewhere or other -- as in the case of public service salaries. Also, the demands of the education and social service programmes following commitments entered into before 1966, were hard to resist without major policy changes which the NLC could not, or did not wish to, contemplate despite its early criticisms of the overambitious nature of Nkrumah's programmes. Between 1962–5 and 1966–9 recurrent spending, at current prices, increased by 35 percent on education and 43 percent on health and social services. Total recurrent public spending increased by 25 percent. And real consumption (in national income terms) increased by as much as a half.

In the event, the main economies in public spending were on the capital account. A large number of proposed projects were cancelled, and others which were already under construction were slowed down, scaled down, or interrupted. Some of these were being, or were to be, financed by supplier credits or Eastern loans already negotiated -- most notably the Accra-Ivory Coast motorway, the Tamalo airport/air base, several ships, the atomic reactor, and many of the Drivici projects. Public investment at current prices fell from £101m. in 1965 to £71m. in 1966, and further to £40m. in 1967. Overall, the reduction in public capital spending between 1962–5 and 1966–9 was 20 percent. At constant prices, domestic fixed investment in the public sector fell by as much as 46 percent.

During the period of stabilisation (1966–7) the total reduction in Central Government spending over spending in 1964–5, was £54m., or £27m. on an annual basis (or £35m. annually for the public sector as a whole -- i.e. including both government and state corporations). The reduction in government spending was accompanied by stagnation in private investment, and the combined effect was a sharp recession which was more intense and lasting than had been foreseen or intended by the stabilisation measures. GDP *per capita* (in real terms) declined for three successive years after 1965. The effect on employment was even more dramatic. In the eighteen months after the coup, at least 70,000 workers lost their jobs. This figure takes into account only workers in paid employment, forming the 'organised' labour market, which the World Bank estimated to have numbered some 600,000 at the time of the coup. Few of these workers were reabsorbed by 1969, and together with new entrants to the labour force they were estimated to have swelled the ranks of the totally unemployed (or only occasionally employed) to about half a million; the unemployment rate in urban areas was thought to be as high as 30 percent. While the reductions in the labour force undoubtedly brought economies in the public sector (without any adverse effect on services or output in most cases), improved the financial position of state farms and other Public Corporations, and reduced overmanning in private industry, a large part of the decline was merely a reflection of reduced public investment, and the closing down of numerous small enterprises. Some of those who lost their jobs found employment on the land, and this had some beneficial effect on cocoa production, but the large shift from town to land that the NLC had hoped to effect did not happen, and indeed could not have happened. While there were undoubtedly serious seasonal shortages of labour in some rural areas, the idea of a mass of urban workers finding regular productive employment on the land was quite impractical. There was some idea of settling workers on state-farm lands turned over to private farming, but even if this could have been achieved, some place had to be found for those already released from employment on the state farms themselves.

Public investment was allowed to fall rather further than originally intended; this was due in part to the drop in revenue (from £142m. in 1965, to £115m. in 1966 and £127m. in 1967), following the decline in economic activity in general, and imports in particular. The success in halving the budget deficit in 1966 was in fact achieved entirely by cuts in investment, since the decrease in recurrent expenditure was offset several times over by the drop in revenue. In the revised budget for the financial year 1966–7, the NLC estimated that balance would be achieved at around the £140m. mark for both revenue and total expenditure. In the final out-turn expenditure was about £10m. more than expected, and revenue £20m. less than expected, producing a deficit of £31m. In the 1967–8 financial year, balance at a much higher level of both revenue and expenditure was forecast, but once again a substantial revenue shortfall forced a downward revision in the expenditure estimates (largely on the capital side) without, however, preventing the budget deficit from widening further; by 1968 the deficit was £35m., compared to £39m. in 1965. However, an important change had been made in the financing of deficits as between the late Nkrumah and the post-Nkrumah years. Whereas formerly deficits were financed by short- or medium-term foreign borrowing and Central Bank borrowing, the NLC deficits could be covered largely, and from 1967–8 entirely, from non-inflationary domestic borrowing, 'revolving' IMF medium-term credits, and inflows of long-term, low-interest or interest-free foreign aid.

Throughout the Nkrumah period the budget had an important influence on the balance of payments; the heavy deficit spending was instrumental in maintaining a high level of demand for imports, while the public investment programme was itself highly import-intensive. However, because of the heavy dependence of government revenue on imports (36 percent of total revenue in 1962–5 was derived from import duties) any attempt to reduce deficit spending caught the government in a spiral of falling expenditure chasing falling revenue; external payments and budget equilibrium could only be attained at much reduced levels of public expenditure and revenue on the one hand, and imports on the other.

Imports after 1965 showed a marked decline (in constant exchange terms)[3] from £188m. in 1965 to £140m. in 1966, and £128m. in both 1967 and 1968; followed by a recovery to £142m. in 1969. In 1966 and 1967, the main restraint came from the reduced budget deficit, which dampened demand for imports of consumer and intermediate goods, and from reduced public investment. After 1967 the main check on the volume of imports came from devaluation — although by 1969 the consequent increase in import prices exerted a new upward push on the import bill. Additional restraints on imports came from a stricter application of import licences and tighter controls over bank credit for import financing.

Reduced imports made possible a reduction in the balance of payments current account deficit, from £80m. in 1965 to £46m. in 1966 and £16m. in 1967 (at constant exchange rates); in the next two years the deficit was almost eliminated, due largely to a substantial recovery in export earnings following an upsurge of cocoa prices; exports had fallen from £126m. in 1965 to £111m. in 1966 and 1967, rising again to £132m. in 1968 and £152m. in 1969. Moreover, whereas the deficit in 1965 had been financed by medium- or short-term foreign credits, the deficits in 1966 and 1967 were largely covered by drawings on the IMF, official aid, and to a lesser extent, by long-term private capital. The new willingness on the part of the West to provide this help thus offered at least some reward for the NLC's friendly overtures and honest stand on the debt issue.

The stabilisation phase of the post-Nkrumah rehabilitation effort was formally completed with the publication of the Two-Year Plan at the beginning of the financial year 1968–9.[4] After the success of the stabilisation policy in terms of its most immediate objectives – containment of the foreign debt and budgetary and external payments stability – and a considered review of spending and other policies, it was now thought possible to resume a modestly expansionary course by encouraging the maximum use of existing productive and infrastructural facilities, supplemented by selective additions and fundamental reforms aimed at encouraging the private sector. Expansion had also become politically more urgent, particularly because of the depressing effect on employment of the stabilisation measures themselves. Nkrumah's counter to the threat of unemployment had been to increase public spending and create jobs, many of which served no obvious productive end. He contained the problem by overburdening the public finances and the balance of payments, and by mortgaging Ghana's future in the hope that it would then be in a better position to repay. The NLC had reversed these priorities, going for budgetary and payments order at the cost of massive unemployment. But it too was unable to ignore the social and political threat from this quarter, and it relaxed its programme of relative austerity as much in response to this factor as from careful calculation of the needs of solidly based growth and development. Moreover, after the end of the period of stabilisation, its attention was increasingly distracted by preparations for a return to civilian rule. In the event, power was transferred smoothly in September 1969 to a civilian administration under Dr. Busia, whose Cabinet included J.H. Mensah – the architect of the old Seven-Year Plan – as the economic supremo; but, at the same time, the civilian administration inherited continued massive unemployment, few positive plans for growth, a budgetary and balance of payments situation coming under renewed pressure, and debt repayments due to rise sharply once again.

2. Economic reforms under the NLC and Busia administrations

Basic economic reforms which were started under the NLC and, with some minor amendments carried on under Busia, concentrated on four areas. The first concerned improvements in the management of the balance of payments, especially imports, by devaluation and related measures, the liberalisation of imports and parallel improvements in their allocation to priority needs, the rationalisation of the structure of import duties, and the introduction of monetary and fiscal incentives to exporters, including an increased producer price for cocoa. Here good results were achieved by the NLC – after a slowish start – but under the Busia administration the reforms collapsed under the massive pressure from imports following ambitious liberalisation, just as the cocoa market went into decline.

The other areas of reform, in which much less impressive results were achieved, were the reallocation of public spending, especially capital spending to more productive purposes; the rehabilitation and restructuring of the state enterprises; and the revitalisation of the rural areas in general, and food production in particular – which was a special concern of the Busia administration.

When the NLC took power, it criticised the Nkrumah investment programme on the grounds that much of it was either of low priority, or insufficiently oriented towards increasing the output of the economy in the short run. Both these criticisms were valid. And yet, in choosing investment projects, the NLC did not do very much better in terms of these same criteria. The distribution of investment between broad sectoral categories under the NLC showed a welcome increase in the relative allocation to agriculture (see Appendix, Table A 6) – thus continuing the gradual trend evident since the Ten-Year Plan. The sharp drop in the share of manufacturing and mining reflected a sensible pause in investment in new state industries. The fall in the share of infrastructure was partly due to the completion in 1966 of the expensive Volta Project. The sharp increase in the shares of the remaining sectors was much less satisfactory, pointing once again to Ghana's long-standing difficulties of containing educational, social, and general government investment to what the economy could finance. These changes do not, of course, give more than a very sketchy picture; nevertheless, in conjunction with evidence on the specific projects that were favoured, they reflect reasonably accurately the preferences of the NLC period.

The allocation of recurrent expenditure under different budget heads during 1966–9 reveals no clear priorities in favour of economic or 'productive' sectors; effectively, the actual amounts spent on various categories were heavily influenced by the curb on imports, so that those programmes which were most heavily dependent on imports tended to suffer most. There was only one exception to this lack of clear priorities, and this was expenditure on defence and internal security. The increased spending on these items, even at a time when overall recurrent expenditure was falling (and even more so the increased outlays on capital account at a time when nearly all other investments were being curtailed) reveals that the NLC was quite capable of exempting its particular 'unproductive' favourites – even in a period of stringency – in just the same way as the former regime had done.

The Busia period was too short for one to be able to draw any meaningful conclusions from the spending pattern; in any case, the lack of statistics makes even a rough estimate impossible. From the limited evidence that is available it looks as if the trend towards favouring agriculture was maintained in both intention and practice.

The early attitude of the NLC towards the growth of state enterprises was one of open hostility. This was based partly on an ideological dislike of state control, echoing in part the old colonial 'minimal government' philosophy in which many of the leading members of the NLC, as well as Dr. Busia, had been reared. A more immediate cause of dislike of state enterprise – and more generally of extensive government involvement in the economy – was the belief that it increased the scope for abuses of all sorts, through state patronage and political pressure; these abuses the NLC, and later also Dr. Busia, were determined to end. On assuming power the NLC thus expected to reduce the role of government in economic affairs, and to give much more scope to the private sector. The initial approach to the problems of the state enterprises was to try to sell them off into private ownership.

But already by mid-1966, the NLC's line had undergone considerable modification. The influence of the Civil Service was one factor. While Western critics continued to attack the concept of state-run industries, or any new major industries in present Ghanaian conditions, the NLC had been persuaded by its own officials – among whom were a number of the leading proponents of state enterprise and industrialisation under the old regime – that Ghana should persevere with them, even if in a modified form. In his Budget Speech in July 1966, General Ankrah put the following case in favour of further industrial development generally:

> First, Ghana needs a rapidly expanding industrial sector in order to provide employment . . . Secondly, industry and its related activities which are able to pay a higher level of wages than the traditional rural sector must contribute an increasing proportion of total employment . . . Thirdly, industry must produce for Ghana more of the commodities that are required to meet the needs of individuals, business enterprises and government. Industry must also earn increasing amounts of foreign exchange with which to buy the goods which we will continue to import from other countries . . . As many industrial enterprises, therefore, as can be established (to achieve these objectives) must be encouraged to start.

On state enterprises in particular, Ankrah said that more had been started than the government could run profitably, and that new efforts should be concentrated on making them work. On the question of ownership the Budget Speech included the following observation:

> We have already offered for sale those public industrial concerns which, in our view, can be more efficiently and profitably managed by private enterprise; but Government is by no means withdrawing from the field of industrial development.

Of the forty-six industrial and commercial state enterprises (excluding state farms, Marketing Boards, and public utilities) established by the Nkrumah regime, only seven were in fact offered for outright sale to the public, while private participation was sought in eleven others. Of the seven offered for sale, two were quite small, and two more of medium size, so that their asset value accounted for a very small proportion of the total assets of the forty-six enterprises under full state ownership at the time of the coup. In the end, the NLC managed to dispose of only three to local industrialists, and in four more foreign private participation was negotiated. Most of the enterprises thus remained in full public ownership.

While the decision to dispose of only some of the state enterprises reflected partly a change of policy by the NLC, the still smaller number actually disposed of illustrates some of the practical obstacles in the way of achieving a successful transfer from public to private (or joint public and private) ownership. One obstacle was financial, in the sense that few Ghanaians had the capital to take over these industries, or wanted to risk it on enterprises whose financial position was as yet shaky. Moreover, the government was particularly interested in attracting experienced companies with know-how and adequate management skills; the most likely candidates, therefore, were expatriate concerns. Considerable interest was indeed shown by foreign enterprises, but it is clear that they did not wish to risk their resources, and wanted particularly favourable terms. Negotiations thus often dragged on without much progress.

It is however likely that many more agreements would have been concluded but for the hostile reception in some intellectual circles in Ghana to a proposed agreement with an American company, Abbott Laboratories, over the sale of the plant and equipment of the State Pharmaceutical Corporation. The terms, which were highly favourable to the American company, set off a general protest against the idea of denationalisation. The NLC did not conclude the agreement; but the affair helped to create an atmosphere of mistrust against other foreign enterprises, leading to a much tougher bargaining stance on Ghana's part. From then on the emphasis was on measures aimed at ensuring better financial, business, and technical management – with contracted outside help where necessary, but leaving enterprises within the public sector.

Progress in improving the performance of state industries since 1966 has been limited, although they appear to have shown a small overall operating surplus since 1968. Returns on capital have remained unsatisfactory, however, though the exact position cannot be assessed accurately because of the failure to keep proper accounts and the confused capital structure of the enterprises. Moveover, the industries are highly import-dependent, and will remain so. The NLC and the Busia regime may thus be said to have spent a great deal of effort and resources in slowly consolidating the industrial legacy left by Nkrumah, when the straightforward cutting of losses might in many cases have been more appropriate in the long run; and indeed, while financial viability for most was within reach by 1972, their net contribution to the economy in the future will remain at best marginal.

The single largest state enterprise at the time of the coup was the State Farms Corporation. Despite the disappointing performance of state farms no attempt was made to abandon them; the programme was, however, reduced in scale: cultivation on seven of the sixty-nine separate farms was abandoned, while another seventeen were transferred from the State Farms Corporation to other public bodies, including thirteen to the Cocoa Division of the Ministry of Agriculture; ten more were taken over by the Ghana Rubber Estate Company, a new enterprise created jointly by the Ghana government and Firestone, to supply the new Firestone Tyre Factory (itself a new joint-enterprise created from a former State Corporation). The rationalisation of state farming around the more promising units offered a real prospect of viability, but the farms were expected to play a relatively minor role in the total agricultural sector, despite the heavy costs which had been incurred when they were founded.

The general state of agriculture in the post-Nkrumah period can be gauged from the modest performance expected from it in the Two-Year Plan assessment. Under the Plan, agricultural production (other than cocoa) was expected to increase by 2.5 percent a year, which was marginally lower than the estimated growth rate in the labour force in this sector. This not only implied lower productivity per man, but also represented a considerably lower rate of growth than in either population or demand, thus increasing the already apparent deficit in food. And, indeed, imports of food, which had risen from £12.6m. in 1965 to £18m. in 1968 (at constant exchange rates) rose still faster after 1968.

The Plan document listed a wide range of measures to improve agriculture, including research, the re-establishment of extension services independent of the state farms, agricultural settlement, mechanisation, credit, irrigation, crop improvement, guaranteed prices, and a rapid build-up in the feeder-road network. All these measures had already been tried before, but this time there was the promise that more manpower and resources would be allocated to them. At the same time, most of the measures were presented only in outline with the details to be filled in after the completion of a comprehensive sectoral study, to be financed by American aid. The Ministry of Economic Affairs dealt rather casually with the arrangements for the sectoral study and it was not started until 1969. Some programmes which had received the go-ahead in anticipation of the study were held up by political and administrative delays, manpower and money shortages; for example, by 1969, only 20 percent of the planned 'high priority' feeder-road programme was completed.

The NLC's agricultural efforts were most vigorous in respect of cocoa -- as previously they had been in the colonial period - and active support for cocoa continued under Dr. Busia. The producer price was raised soon after the coup, from £75 per ton to £84 per ton, and then once again to £122 per ton for the 1966--7 main crop season (October--September). The supply of pesticides to farmers was increased several fold; the subsidies on spraying equipment, which had been withdrawn in the period of cocoa glut in the early 1960s, were reintroduced; the extension service, which had been run down, was strengthened; supervised control of swollen shoot was stepped up again; and experimental plantings with new higher-yielding tree varieties were initiated, followed in 1970 by a major programme of replanting. However, the effect of most of these measures on output could not be felt for four to five years, and of the replanting programme for seven to ten years. During 1966–9, and also in 1970–71, the effects of the neglect of cocoa in the first half of the sixties had worked themselves through and output declined by some 20 percent over the 1962–5 period. Exports also fell, from an average of 425,000 tons in 1962–5 to an average of 340,000 tons in 1966–9 and 350,000 tons in 1970–71. However, as had happened before, reduced exports were accompanied by increased prices, giving Ghana somewhat larger export earnings in 1966–9 (averaging £73m.) than in 1962–5 (£72m.) despite the much reduced quantity exported. Particularly high earnings in 1968 and 1969 contributed much to Ghana's ability to maintain balance of payments equilibrium in spite of increased public spending, imports and other external payments, including debt-service charges. Conversely, the simultaneous fall in exports and prices in 1970–71 made Ghana's position extremely difficult again just at the time when the breathing space provided through the second debt rescheduling agreement concluded by the NLC was coming to an end.

The overall record of post-Nkrumah rehabilitation efforts under the first two successor regimes may be summarised in the following terms. In the economic field the NLC was an essentially negative government. This was appropriate in the year or two of severe financial and balance of payments constraint following the overthrow of Nkrumah, but the relative lack of initiative and interest in new development policies following the short-term success of the stabilisation measures proved a major hindrance. Ghana's hard core problems inherited from the Nkrumah, or even earlier, periods required not only imaginative policies but also a major political effort to mobilise resources and to counteract growing popular disenchantment and restlessness. The NLC could provide neither of these. The Busia administration started on a much more positive note than the one on which the NLC saw out its last months in office; and brought some new sense of purpose to the development effort. But it had little chance to prove itself before it had to concentrate its efforts on new emergency measures to deal with a downturn in Ghana's balance of payments. Moreover, it had to take on Ghana's creditors once again and almost immediately, in new rounds of negotiations, but in circumstances more difficult than those which the NLC had faced in 1968.

3. Efforts to reschedule the foreign debt

Efforts to reach a final agreement on a rescheduling of Ghana's short-term and medium-term debts – which stood at around £40m. and £155m. respectively at the beginning of 1966 – started within weeks of the coup and went on almost continuously until mid-1967, to be resumed in mid-1968 and again early in the Busia administration. There were four major rounds of international meetings all told, at which four multilateral agreements were reached, two interim, and one so-called 'final', but which was followed by yet another 'interim' agreement. In between, bilateral discussions went on for much of the time, in Accra or in different creditor capitals, either in preparation for, or as a follow-up to, the main international rounds. In addition negotiations with some creditor governments, principally those of Eastern bloc countries, with several major private creditors, were conducted on an exclusively bilateral basis. In all, the debt issue took a considerable slice out of the time of Ghana's economic ministers and senior officials, becoming a permanent fixture on the agenda in meetings with political or government representatives of a score of industrial countries. At the same time, bilateral and multilateral negotiations on aid were taking place (see Section 4).

In announcing its intention to honour its debt obligations to the full, the NLC had expected to come to a speedy and reasonable arrangement with its creditors. This did prove to be the case in respect of short-term debts, and a *de facto* moratorium on medium-term credits was accepted without protest; but the negotiations on a satisfactory long-term arrangement proved extremely difficult, and ended in failure.

Immediately after the coup there was a strong feeling, particularly among Ghanaians in exile, who had had no personal stake in, but had observed from afar, the corruption and malpractices associated with supplier credits, that Ghana should repudiate most, if not all, the Nkrumah debts. There was a similar mood within the Ghana Civil Service, particularly among the younger officials, many of whom had watched their political masters succumbing, willingly or unwillingly, to the high-pressure sales techniques of foreign suppliers.

General Ankrah considered a repudiation to be immoral, and made his views known in the most categorical terms; he thought that his attitude would be a positive factor in any future negotiations with creditors – but it may be doubted whether he had at the time fully appreciated the extent of Ghana's debts, or had any conception of the positions that Ghana's creditors might adopt. Ankrah's view was shared by the majority of his NLC colleagues, although from less high-minded motives. In any case, the decision to honour the debts was taken largely on political grounds, before a careful assessment could be made of the extent of the debt burden, or the circumstances in which the different obligations had been accepted. E.N. Omaboe, the Chief Statistician under Nkrumah, who had to the end publicly decried the policies of the former regime, was appointed Chairman of the NLC Economic Committee, becoming the effective architect of NLC economic policy; he too was against repudiation, on grounds of economic necessity. The decision certainly made economic management in the early months of the NLC administration easier. But once the creditors had come to appreciate the gentlemanly attitude of the new regime to its debt obligations, much of the uncertainty that would otherwise have surrounded their dealings with Ghana was removed, and their bargaining position made even stronger than it already was. It is idle to speculate on the likely course of events if Ghana had repudiated the medium-term debts, and on whether any long-term advantage could have been secured. But it is clear that a more guarded and non-committal attitude to the debt – until a full review could be carried out – would have offered considerable tactical advantages after Ghana had made its undertaking to honour commercial credits in full and thus secured the continued flow of essential imports, preventing also a further downgrading in its international rating for export credit insurance cover. It is interesting that of the three countries that made a prompt positive response to General Ankrah's request, in March 1966, for immediate help of £15m. for essential imports, two – Canada and the United States – were only minor creditors; the other, West Germany – which was a major creditor – had already expressed its willingness to provide some relief in the last months of Nkrumah's regime and discussions happened to be in progress at the time of the coup.

In April of 1966, Ghana managed to get grudging agreement from major importers to whom payments on 180-day credit were substantially in arrears to continue supplies on previous terms, on the understanding that from then on payments on new supplies would be made when due, while the arrears would be cleared in full, on a non-discriminatory basis, as and when foreign exchange became available. Having obtained this agreement, Ghana turned to the IMF for help with its stabilisation programme, with both advice and stand-by credit. In addition, Ghana wanted the IMF to use its good offices with potential donors and with Ghana's creditors. In its presentation to the

IMF, Ghana claimed that, in order to avoid a catastrophic recession, it needed to import during 1966 £125m. worth of 'essential' commodities (other than capital equipment already in the pipeline under old credit arrangements) – compared with £140m. in such imports in 1965. It claimed, also, that after meeting debt payments on medium- and long-term credits, and other unavoidable charges, its available foreign exchange for the remainder of 1966 was no more than £15m. (excluding offers of aid of £4.4m. already made). While the request was being considered, Ghana also made preliminary soundings among its major creditors with a view to starting negotiations on debt relief. There was no action on their part until the IMF findings on Ghana's needs became available in mid-May. The IMF concluded that Ghana could get by with some £25m. less in imports during 1966 than it had claimed but that even so considerable external assistance in one form or another would be required; it agreed to an immediate stand-by credit of £14m. (for 3–5 years at 2–3 percent interest). Following this, the British government agreed to convene an early meeting of officials from the fourteen IMF members to whom Ghana was indebted on medium- or long-term credits.

The first full conference on Ghana's debts was held in London at the beginning of June, i.e. fourteen weeks after the downfall of Nkrumah. Two decisions were reached. First, Ghana was granted a moratorium on all debt payments on supplier credits until the autumn, by which time permanent solution to the debt problem to be worked out. Second, Britain agreed to call a full-scale conference in the autumn; in the meantime the IMF and IBRD were to help in a review of Ghana's debts and in the preparations for the conference. The creditors met in London, without Ghana but with the IMF as an observer, in October (when a *de facto* extension of the June moratorium emerged) and again in November. The full meeting with Ghana was held the following month, and an agreement in principle on rescheduling a part of the debt was reached on 10 December, thirty-one weeks after the initial London meeting.

Apart from representatives from Ghana, the IMF, and IBRD, the meeting was attended by officials from Britain (in the chair) and West Germany – the two main creditors – and the Netherlands, Italy, Japan, Norway, and Switzerland, all with £1m. or more in outstanding debt; Belgium, Israel, and US, all with less than £1m.; and Australia and Canada, with less than £100,000. Two other IMF members, France (a major creditor) and Egypt (a minor creditor), were not represented. The agreement covered all medium-term debts (those of over one year and up to twelve years maturity) contracted before 23 February 1966, and due (including arrears) between 1 June 1966 (i.e. the date of the first London meeting) and 31 December 1968. The amount involved was £56m. Of this, 20 percent was to be paid in the eighteen months from July 1967 to December 1968; this was to be followed by a grace period of 2½ years during which only interest was to be paid; the remaining 80 percent was to be paid off in rising instalments over eight years, starting with 2½ percent of the total on 1 July 1971. Interest on the deferred principal was to be agreed in bilateral negotiations. The first of these was concluded with Britain, the major creditor, in February 1967, covering debts of £22m. principal and £3m. interest. An interest rate of just under 6 percent was imposed on the deferred debt, both principal and interest. The average interest eventually negotiated with other donors was 6 percent, or a fraction higher than that charged by Britain.

The overall agreement was a compromise between the initial creditors' offer (25 percent of the debt to be paid between 1 January 1966 and 31 December 1968, followed by two years' grace and settlement of the rest over four years) and Ghana's request (15 percent over three years, then five years' grace, then 85 percent over twelve years, with very low interest on the deferred principal). The effective relief obtained by Ghana for the three years 1966–68 worked out at £37m. (from £56m. to £19m.); but payments on supplier credits were to rise rapidly again after only two years, from £11.8m. in 1968, to £21.2m. in 1969, and £17.4m. in 1970 (se schedules below). Moreover, as a consequence of the high interest rates imposed on the deferred debt, the total debt outstanding was increased by £20m.

The delay in coming to an agreement and the 'interim' nature of the deal offered by Ghana's creditors – in contrast to the ease with which the short-term debt agreement was reached – were due, in large measure, to the fact that this time Ghana had to deal – collectively – with governments rather than individual private concerns. For private companies who lend to bankrupt concerns, the inevitable consequence is commercial loss. However, in so far as most of Ghana's credits had been covered by official guarantee against default or late payment, it was the creditor governments – or the agencies which provided cover – who stood to lose by Ghana's failure to meet its debts on time. In negotiating with governments, rather than private concerns, Ghana was at a serious disadvantage, particularly if the creditor governments were determined to minimise their own losses on the insured credits. While Ghana's case was sympathetically considered, it had few real friends among the creditors. Of the main creditors, Britain, the Netherlands, Italy, and Japan were in no mood to give away anything that was not strictly necessary and France did not even attend the debt talks; only Germany took a moderately encouraging stance. Ghana's main sympathisers were to be found among the smaller creditors, especially Canada and the United States. While the small sums these had at stake permitted them to adopt a more liberal attitude, it also gave them little scope for setting a positive example. In the end, the concessions which were made to Ghana were prompted largely by the creditors' desire to avoid forcing the NLC into a repudiation; this none of them wanted because of the possible reaction among countries in which their stake, in terms of both debt and general commercial interest, was greater.

Ghana was handicapped, also, by the fact that Britain was a reluctant 'chairman' – a duty that devoled on it by virtue of the established convention that the biggest creditor, rather than an independent arbitrator, should be in the chair. Britain was in a difficult position. As the largest creditor it had the greatest stake in preventing default. At the same time, it was Ghana's most important trading partner, and its investment interests were bigger by far than those of any of the other creditors, and therefore it had the greatest stake also in ensuring that Ghana's economy could function normally. But if it took a lead in offering generous terms it would have to meet most of the cost; and Britain was particularly anxious at the time to minimise commitments which imposed any balance of payments costs. It preferred to come to some temporary arrangement during which Ghana's progress could be observed. As one official was to remark at a later round of the debt negotiations: with Ghana's dependence on cocoa anything could happen, even a price boom big enough to make its debt-burden quite manageable. When it came to setting an interest rate on the deferred debt, the British government took the view that this should correspond to the interest charges on the original contracts. There was no real justification for this rate, although it was claimed that it allowed creditors some compensation through interest payments on the part of the debt not insured through ECGD, and also allowed ECGD to recover the interest charges it had to incur on borrowing to meet its own domestic obligations, following rescheduling. Even though British interest rates had been among the highest, most other creditors followed Britain in setting a high rate on the deferred debt; no one was prepared to cross-subsidise payments to other creditors. While Britain's dilemma over the debt deal was understandable, it nevertheless contributed to Ghana's difficulties in reaching an agreement, both this time round and in later negotiations.

Ghana's tactics in the 1966 negotiations may also be questioned. The NLC concentrated on getting the best possible rescheduling terms, having accepted responsibility for the entire Nkrumah debt – with the exception of the Drivici debt which was a special case and not included in the rescheduling negotiations (see below). While many foreign observers accused some of the foreign firms of dubious practices in getting credit contracts, or short-changing Ghana on these contracts, the NLC was careful to avoid joining such a witch-hunt, and concentrated instead on the role played by Ghanaians in the debacles of the Nkrumah period. Ghana's line allowed creditor governments to escape rather easily from the consequences of their own carelessness in the matter of accepting insurance cover in these credit contracts. Moreover, Ghana made it easier for them to save face by not exposing the inadequacy of the way in which Ghana's creditworthiness had been assessed, and not insisting more forcefully that they should now accept the consequences of their own mistakes.

When the NLC came to power it showed open hostility towards communist countries, which manifested itself, among other things, in the explusion of Russian and Chinese technicians and the unilateral cancellation of a number of Eastern projects. At the time, debts owed to these two countries were subject to a two-year moratorium which Nkrumah negotiated with them just before his overthrow; a *de facto* moratorium applied to the debts of other Eastern countries, except Yugoslavia. Although the NLC showed little inclination to maintain friendly relations with Eastern countries, it accepted the advice of the IMF and Omaboe, amongst others, to come to some formal understanding on the future of the Eastern debts -- if only to safeguard the potentially viable Eastern projects still under construction – as well as on the bilateral trade agreements, which in some cases had worked to Ghana's disadvantage.

The Eastern debt issue was not particularly urgent. Only some 20 percent of all medium-term debts was involved, and repayments were stretched over a longer period than on the original Western schedule. However, once the negotiations with Western creditors were out of the way after the London agreement of December 1966, negotiations were initiated with Yugoslavia, and with Russia as the main Eastern creditor. Agreement with Yugoslavia was reached at the first try, in March 1967; Ghana asked for, and obtained, a rescheduling on the same terms as those negotiated with its Western creditors. Negotiations with Russia proved more difficult, and no agreement was reached at the first attempt. Later during the year, with the return of more cordial relations with Russia, agreement was reached, again on similar terms to those at the London conference. Other East European countries followed suit, except for Czechoslovakia, whose debts were unilaterally rescheduled; no arrangements were made with China. Although the two sets of rescheduling terms – in respect of deferment and of the method of imposing interest on the deferred debt – were almost identical, the original difference in interest rates on Western and Eastern contracts meant that a much smaller relative interest burden was added in the latter case. The additional interest on the deferred debt of almost £12m. came to less than £2m., or 16 percent compared to 42 percent on the deferred debt to Western countries.

Ghana took the strongest line in debt negotiations with Drivici, the Rumanian-born financier and industrialist who had inspired some of the most ill-advised projects under Nkrumah. Before the coup Ghana had signed contracts for 14 projects worth £70m. with various companies, based in West Germany and Switzerland, with which Drivici was associated, and Ghana had already made over a total of £14m. in down payments. At the time of the coup the 'Swiss' projects, which had not yet been started, were cancelled, while work on several others was suspended until their viability and the circumstances in which they had been signed were investigated. In September 1967 agreement was reached between the NLC and Drivici for work to resume on seven of the original projects, the rest being cancelled or abandoned. The sum of £14m. already paid by Ghana was credited to the cost of completing the projects which were to be continued. The balance required – £6m. – was to be found by Drivici in the form of equity investment. While even then Ghana did not obtain value for its original payment of £14m., the debts contracted on the Drivici projects were at least settled without the need to make any further payments.

The four different agreements reached on the medium-term debts during 1966 and 1967 – with Western creditors, the Eastern 'bloc', Yugoslavia, and the Drivici companies – together with the stand-by credits from the IMF, provided sufficient relief for Ghana to achieve the main aims of its stabilisation programme. The full extent of the relief can be gauged from the fact that in the two years Ghana had to pay out £11m. in debt service charges, instead of the £50m. originally scheduled on all medium- and long-term credits. Taking into account the short-term debt, the overall burden was reduced from £90m. to £11m. Despite this, stabilisation could be achieved only at the cost of a recession more severe than had been expected.

In 1968, as Ghana moved into its phase of cautious expansion, it was clear that further outside help was required. The debt was once again looming on the horizon; the room for manoeuvre gained by the various agreements would soon be lost as a result of the sharply increased debt-service payments scheduled from 1969 onwards, unless further relief could be obtained, particularly on the Western medium-term debt.

It had been recognised at the end of the London conference of 1966 that the agreements then reached offered no more than a temporary solution. In the spring of 1968 Ghana asked for, and obtained, another IMF stand-by credit of £4.2m., and this cleared the way for another approach to its Western creditors for another debt conference. Britain agreed to convene a meeting, and a second conference was held in London in October, twenty-two months after the last one. It was attended by representatives of Britain, West Germany and the Netherlands, (75 percent of the medium-term debt was now owed to these three); and Norway, Belgium, Italy, Israel, Japan, and the US. This time France sent an observer, but Australia and Canada (whose small outstanding credits required no further action) and Switzerland (whose contracts had been cancelled by the Drivici agreement) were no longer involved. An agreement was reached involving debts originally due between 1 January 1969 and 30 June 1972. Of these 20 percent was to be paid in rising instalments during the period, followed by a two-year grace period and payment of the remaining 80 percent over seven-and-a-half years starting on 1 July 1974. Interest on the deferred debt was again left to bilateral negotiations, although the creditors jointly recommended that no more than 6 percent should be charged by any one of them; and this was the effective rate which was agreed in the bilateral negotiations which followed. Ghana was moderately happy about the agreement as a whole, but bitterly disappointed by the interest rate imposed on the deferred debt. It had asked for a maximum of 3 percent and got 6 percent, adding another £13m. in interest charges to the total oustanding debt.

Between December 1966 and October 1968 the position of the creditors had hardened considerably. They expressed some disappointment with Ghana's progress, especially in view of the aid and debt relief they had provided. As far as they were concerned, therefore, the latest rescheduling had been generous – and final. The original debt schedule on the Nkrumah medium-term debt to Western countries, together with the new schedules agreed at the London conferences of 1966 and 1968, are shown below. From this it can be seen that the combined effect of the two rescheduling agreements was to provide generous relief on the medium-term debt due for payment in the NLC period. (But, besides this debt, there remained the long-term and Eastern debts.) Thereafter, including all payments on credits of more than one year's maturity, the Busia administration faced a rise in the debt burden from an estimated £10m. in 1969, to an estimated £18m. in 1970 and again in 1971, and £25m. each in the following two years.

The debt relief and new aid provided for 1968 and 1969 allowed the NLC to hand over power in an expansionary phase. In 1969 GDP per head in real terms showed the first rise for five years. But the increase was made possible partly by sacrificing the budgetary and balance of payments stability achieved earlier. It was clear by August, when the budget was presented, that in the second half of 1969 public spending (including debt payments) and imports could not be held to levels that Ghana's domestic revenue, foreign exchange earnings, and net aid flows would permit, without yet again jeopardising growth.

Table 6.1 Western supplier credits: new payments schedules, 1966 and 1968.
(in £m. at constant exchange rate)

	1966	1967	1968	1969	1970	1971	1972	1973
Original schedule	13.7	20.2	22.3	17.9	14.4	10.9	7.0	5.0
Post-1966 schedule	—	3.2	11.8	21.2	17.4	16.0	13.8	12.0
Post-1968 schedule	—	—	—	6.0	8.1	9.5	14.3	14.7
Actual payments (up to end of 1968)	(4.0)	3.0	12.5	—	—	—	—	—
Actual payments (post-1969 schedule) all debts over one year (excl. IMF)	—	—	—	(10.0)	(18.0)	(18.0)	(24.0)	(26.0)

Notes: ( ) Estimate

▬ Years to which debt rescheduling applies.

Sources: Information supplied by IBRD and US AID (Accra)

In its first Budget presentation, therefore, the new Busia administration asked for immediate additional long-term refinancing aid to cover the debts due in the current financial year (1969–70) and for a reopening of negotiations on the whole debt question. Towards the end of the NLC period J.H. Mensah, who had become the new Commissioner for Finance, had started a campaign criticising the attitude of Ghana's creditors, particularly Western creditors. For the first time senior members of the administration began to state publicly that Ghana might be forced to take some form of unilateral action to ease the debt burden. Moreover, Mensah's case for further relief now switched to criticism of the role played by suppliers in the amassing of the debt. Instead of parading Ghana's follies in accepting the contractor deals, the emphasis turned to the 'sharp practices' and irresponsibility of the foreign suppliers; and the lack of responsibility shown by Eastern governments who had been involved directly, and Western governments who had provided guarantees. A case-by-case review of contracts, and selective repudiation of these where Ghana had not obtained value for money, was now strongly hinted at.

The new 'hard' line from Mensah was supplemented by a softer line from Busia, whose appeal to Western creditors emphasised Ghana's need for help to ensure the success of its return to democratic, civilian rule. The two leaders visited London, Paris and Washington in October 1969 to argue Ghana's case. A special appeal was made to Britain (to which Ghana owed 40 percent of the outstanding debt on supplier credits) to convene a new debt conference. Britain responded by offering a refinancing loan of £1.75m. towards the debt payments due in 1969–70. But it was cool towards the idea of a further conference. When Ghana protested the following March at Britain's delay in calling a new conference, Britain declared its agreement in principle, but refused to take any action until a 'proper case' could be presented by Ghana.

Ghana's case was presented in May 1970. A meeting of thirteen creditor country representatives in London agreed to reopen negotiations in early July. In its presentation in May, Ghana stated its displeasure at the treatment it had received, comparing this with the generous treatment which had been accorded to Indonesia in similar circumstances. Ghana put its total debt, as of 31 May 1969 – the figures used were those prepared by the NLC for the donors' Paris meeting that year – at £345m., or £90m. more than at the time of the 1966 coup. The sum was broken down as follows: £145m. in medium-term debt (of which £105m. was in respect of supplier credits);

£130m. in long-term loans; and £70m. in short-term debts and IMF obligations. Ghana requested a rescheduling of the debt owed on suppliers credits along the lines of that offered on the Indonesian debt, which were similar to the terms of standard IDA credits. It proposed a ten-year grace period, with payments spread over forty years and a maximum interest rate of 2 percent on the deferred principal; alternatively, the forty-year payment period could be cut to thirty years if more long-term loans at low interest were offered.

The formal negotiations with Ghana opened in London in July, with Britain again taking the chair. The British representative, speaking on behalf of all the creditors present, expressed disappointment that Ghana had asked for the debt question to be reopened. He rejected the claim that the debt service burden, in 1970 and 1971 at least, was one which Ghana could not meet. In respect of the Western supplier credits this view was certainly justified. However, Ghana's concern was with the problem over a longer time perspective -- it wished to get a settlement that could be final in reality and not merely in name. At the same time, as far as 1970 and 1971 were concerned, Ghana had to consider its total servicing commitments, which were put at £43m. and £35m. respectively. A complete moratorium on supplier credits for ten years would thus have helped in the critical short run as well, by giving relief on 50 percent of total payments due on medium- and long-term credits, and making it easier to meet IMF obligations and to reduce, by at least a small amount, the outstanding short-term debt. The creditors recognised that some immediate relief was, after all, justified, and offered concessions on 25 percent of the amount due on supplier credits between July 1970 and June 1972. In the end they improved their offer to 50 percent of the debt then due, leaving each creditor to select one of three alternative methods: a refinancing loan with a minimum grant element of 61 percent; a straightforward ten-year deferment without any additional interest charge; or additional aid, also with a minimum 6 percent grant-element. Ghana accepted provisionally, and an agreement on these terms was initialled on the understanding that another conference would be convened before mid-1972, and that for that occasion a neutral arbitrator would be appointed. In the meantime Ghana was expected to continue bilateral negotiations with the various creditors to work out detailed agreements with each. Once again the creditors had followed the precedent set at the 1966 conference of not committing themselves to an effectively permanent arrangement.

Britain chose to make its contribution to the latest London

settlement in the form of a refinancing loan of £3.5m. However, disagreement arose about the interpretation of the London settlement, which Ghana considered as having provided the minimum terms which creditors were prepared to negotiate. Discussions held in December, first in Accra and then in London, failed to produce agreement. Ghana demanded that relief should apply to the interest due on the debt which had previously been deferred, a claim that Britain firmly rejected, and in which it was supported by a number of other creditors. It was not until July 1971 – a full year after the London conference – that Ghana reluctantly accepted the British refinancing loan on British terms. At the same time Mensah once again expressed the Ghana governments displeasure at its treatment and questioned Ghana's ability to meet its obligations in 1972.

During 1971 Ghana's financial and balance of payments situation deteriorated rapidly. The combined effect of the renewed economic expansion of 1969 and 1970, import liberalisation, and the sharp decline in cocoa exports in 1971, brought a surge of imports on which payments could not be made. The short-term debt, largely through arrears on 180-day trade credits and other payments, shot up to some £65m. by the end of the year. In November, Busia again asked for help, visiting London and Washington. At home, the government introduced new austerity measures, which included, early in January 1972, a massive devaluation (of 48 percent) to stem the tide of imports.

On 13 January the Busia administration was removed by a new military coup, headed by Colonel Acheampong. The new regime – the National Redemption Council – promptly announced unilateral measures on Ghana's debt. The short-term debt was to be honoured when Ghana's foreign exchange position allowed; also no further imports on 180-day credit would be sought. The supplier credits accepted under Nkrumah would be re-examined and, where the circumstances under which they had been accepted were questionable, repudiated. The debt owed on contracts to four British companies was repudiated forthwith. All medium-term credits (except to the IMF) which were to be honoured would be rescheduled roughly on the terms proposed by Mensah at the 1970 London talks, i.e. a ten-year grace period and a forty-year repayment period; but the interest obligation increased under the 1966 and 1968 rescheduling agreements was rejected.

As a result of the NRC's action insurance-cover on exports to Ghana was withdrawn by all the main creditor countries. Aid negotiations were interrupted, with only a few donors – the US, West Germany, and the World Bank – prepared to contemplate further support. Formally, the creditors have looked upon the Acheampong measures as proposals rather than a *fait accompli*, and a counter-offer, more generous than before, was made after a creditors meeting in October 1972. Its terms were a five-year grace period, followed by repayment over fifteen years, normalisation of trade, and resumed long-term financial aid. The offer was communicated to Ghana by a World Bank mission in November; but Ghana had made no formal reply by spring 1973.

Time must elapse before the full impact of Acheampong's action can be assessed. So far no collapse of the kind that the NLC had feared in 1966 has taken place, although the financial and debt circumstances were then little different from those in 1972. Acheampong appears to be in no hurry to seek a new agreement with Ghana's creditors. It is unclear how long he could survive on a policy of self-reliance and anti-foreign sentiment – as evidenced by the nationalisation of foreign companies, including the Ashanti gold-mines – particularly if the World Bank lost interest. As for Ghana's main creditors, they have failed, perhaps irrevocably, to avoid the debt repudiation which had been their primary fear throughout the negotiations with the NLC and the Busia governments.

4. Aid from the West

Under both the NLC and the Busia administrations aid agreements were concluded with Western governments and international financial organisations only, although in 1966 and 1967 some £9m. in Eastern credits, in the pipeline at the time of the coup, was also used. Reliance on the West was largely a matter of political and ideological preference, although the NLC also considered that the West offered unrivalled expertise, and was a bigger source of capital, including the only source of private investment capital on which it was hoped to put a much greater emphasis.[5]

Ghana got a quick response from Canada, the United States, and West Germany, who promised £4.5m. in commodity aid within a month of the coup; but negotiations with Britain were initially unsuccessful. Ghana had asked to be allowed to spend the unused portion of the £5m. Volta loan on commodity imports, or on an electricity distribution scheme related to the Volta Project. This scheme was taken up by West Germany in September, and further discussions on the unused portion of the British loan were discontinued. Britain's first offer of aid (for £4m.) was not made until after the first meeting of donors organised by the IMF in May 1967, and not signed until that August.

The first multilateral aid meeting, held in Paris and following closely on the creditors' meeting in December 1966 in London, was attended by Britain, Canada, Denmark, France, West Germany, Italy, Japan, US, the IBRD, and UNDP, with a DAC observer. Of the governments present, only Denmark was not involved as a creditor; while the most notable absentees among the creditors were the Netherlands and Norway. Ghana estimated that its import requirements for 1967 would be £144m., leaving an estimated balance of payments gap of between £42m. and £47m., which was put as the minimum aid requirement for the year. At the meeting Canada and Denmark made offers of support, but detailed negotiations with them and other countries represented were to follow on a bilateral basis. A second meeting of donors took place in Accra in September 1967, attended by the same countries. The meeting agreed that current aid flows were below the needs required to make Ghana's stabilisation efforts succeed, and urged that the disbursement of aid already offered should be speeded up. It also agreed that another meeting should take place in 1968. By the end of 1967, Britain, Canada, Denmark, Germany, and the US had made firm aid commitments of £19.5m., and an IMF stand-by of £9m. brought the total up to £28.5m. However, during 1967, only £3.8m. in aid was actually disbursed; plus £6.3m. from an IMF 'compensatory finance' loan made at the end of 1966, and the stand-by credit, this made a total of almost £20m. in long- and medium-term finance. It allowed Ghana to buy imports up to £129m., instead of the £144m. it had considered desirable.

The third meeting was held in Paris in February 1968; this time the Netherlands, Norway, and Switzerland were represented, in addition to the countries taking part in the earlier meetings. At this meeting Ghana expressed its disappointment with aid and other forms of relief received so far. It claimed that the recession consequent on the stabilisation measures was more serious than had been expected, and blamed the slow rate at which aid was disbursed – £11m. in 1966–7 – for having forced a reduction in public spending by more than was planned, and in imports to below the desired level. There was some justification in this view, which appears to be confirmed by the trend in maintenance imports essential to production, which rose only in the latter part of 1967 in line with the build-up of commodity aid (see Table 6.2). But the figures can be used also to show that the bigger problem stemmed from the NLC's failure – after an initial policy of boosting such imports, to attract political support – to contain consumer imports sufficiently to make room for essential maintenance imports. As can be seen from the table, Ghana did manage to contain total current imports (i.e. excluding capital goods) to the level advised for 1966 by the IMF; but maintenance imports in that year fell from the already inadequate level of 1965, rising only in 1967, with most of the increase coming in the second half of the year. Imports of consumer goods fell more sharply, by 30 percent between 1965 and 1966, and then again following devaluation in mid-1967. However, since the surge in consumer imports in 1965 had been exceptional, the figures for 1964 give a better picture of the level of imports to which the population had become accustomed. Moreover, large stocks (especially of Eastern goods) remained from the imports bought in 1965, and the NLC may with some justification be accused of having pandered to the Ghanaian preference for Western goods, which it shared.

Table 6.2 Ghana's import structure, 1964–1967. (in £m. at constant exchange rates)

Year	Consumer Imports	Maintenance imports (other than building materials)	Total Current Imports	Commodity aid (Western)
1964	40.8	27.6	109.0	–
1965	54.9	32.1	140.0	–
1966	38.8	28.2	104.0	3.3 (75% food)
1967	36.8	36.9	104.0	6.5

Sources: As for Tables A 9 and 6.3.

Among other factors making for a deeper and more prolonged recession than expected were continued problems in rehabilitating the state enterprises, the failure of labour redeployment efforts, and, most seriously, a sharp decline in cocoa export proceeds resulting from a simultaneous drop in output and export prices. Ghana's problems thus had different origins: some were the consequence of failures of NLC policy and some of events beyond the NLC's control; but all, at least in part, were the backlog of problems from before 1966. Aid commitments reached their peak in 1968, particularly in the first half of the year which accounted for 70 percent of the total; thereafter they fell off rapidly (see Table 6.3). The decline thus came just as Ghana was moving from stabilisation into a phase of planned expansion. With the crisis over, Ghana's claim for special consideration appeared less evident to most donors – particularly in view of the aid pipeline that amounted to nearly £30m. in mid-1968. Only the US, Britain (reluctantly), the World Bank, Canada, and Germany made firm commitments in the two years from mid-1968 to mid-1970 (and France made a preliminary offer). Ghana's most enthusiastic supporters appeared to be the World Bank, the US, and West Germany. Ghana had perhaps few pressing claims for aid in competition with other developing countries, which were either much poorer, or had demonstrated their ability to use aid effectively, or both. That Ghana's treatment at the hands of the donors was less generous once its immediate crisis was over further illustrates its marginal political importance, not justifying, it would seem, the sort of 'generosity' extended to some other countries -- most notably Indonesia – which had got themselves into similar financial and payments difficulties. Yet this lack of political weight might have been offset if Ghana's ability to improve its performance had been more forcefully demonstrated. As it was, its stabilisation measures had given some proof of determination to improve performance over that achieved in the later Nkrumah years, but most donors, particularly Britain, remained cautious about its capacity to implement a sound development programme.

Moreover, once Ghana's immediate crisis was over, the debt, particularly its unequal distribution between different Western creditors, complicated aid negotiations. The largest creditors were keenest on a solution which would help to prevent default. At the same time, the more generous the terms of the debt settlement, the greater the burden they would have to bear, at least in the short run. However, if Ghana received substantial amounts of aid the 'cost' to the creditors would be partly offset by a faster rate of debt-repayment. Thus, the United States - whose political commitment to Ghana was stronger than that of most others – wished to see a generous debt settlement and a sizeable volume of new aid. In that way, the US, as a small creditor, could be certain that it was not merely financing debt-service payments to other creditors. Britain, on the other hand, while prepared to give a reasonable volume of aid, wanted, as the largest creditor, a less generous debt settlement; or a more generous settlement, with other countries bearing a large part of the burden. West Germany was in a

Table 6.3 New aid commitments and disbursements, 1966–1970 [1] ($m)

	Commitments					Disbursements (gross)				
	1966	1967	1968	1969	1970	1966	1967	1968	1969	1970
Britain										
Programme	–	11.2	11.5	13.0	10.3	–	0.1	12.2	11.6	12.7
Canada										
Programme	2.0	2.0	2.0	–	3.0	2.0	2.0	2.0	–	3.0
Project	–	–	–	7.0	†	–	–	–	0.5	†
Denmark										
Project	–	2.7	–	–	–	–	–	0.2	1.0	†
Germany(West)										
Programme	5.0	3.0	3.6	–	†	3.2	1.8	2.9	3.8	†
Project	5.0	3.4	2.5	–	†	–	–	5.0	1.6	†
Italy										
Programme	–	–	10.0	2.0	†	–	–	–	–	†
US										
Programme	7.5	30.5	34.9	18.0	†	6.2	6.7	18.5	26.4	†
Project	–	2.0	–	–	†	–	–	0.9	0.8	†
World Bank/ IDA										
Project	–	–	10.0	12.3	†	–	–	–	6.6	†
Total programme	14.5	46.7	62.0	33.0	†	11.4	10.6	35.6	41.8	†
Total project	5.0	8.1	12.5	19.3	†	–	–	6.1	10.5	†
Grand Total	19.5	54.8	74.5	52.3	( )	11.4	10.6	41.7	52.3	67.2
Sterling Equivalent [2]	7.0	19.5	26.6	18.7	( )	4.0	3.8	14.9	18.7	24.0

Notes:
† No separate breakdown available, included in grand total.
1. Includes only commitments and disbursements made since the February 1966 coup.
2. Sterling/dollar exchange rate as at February 1966.

Sources: Ministry of Economic Affairs (External Aid Division) Accra, and Official Press releases.

position somewhat similar to Britain; the other main creditors were mainly interested in preventing default at least cost to themselves.

An additional complication was the internal conflict of interest within the governments of both Britain and West Germany, where the Treasury and Ministry of Finance pressed for a debt solution most favourable to the *creditors*, while the aid agencies were interested in solutions rather more favourable to Ghana, if for no other reason than to prevent aid funds being absorbed in debt-relief.

It is not surprising, therefore, that these conflicting creditor interests, added to Ghana's lack of persuasive long-term claims to help, resulted in Ghana receiving just enough to allow it to continue honouring its debt obligations. This arrangement, let off rather lightly some of the bigger European creditors, notably France, Italy and the Netherlands. The US, Britain, and Germany shouldered most of the burden of the West's support for the NLC.

Notes

1. Budget Speech, 20 July 1966.
2. *Report on the Structure and Remuneration of the Public Services in Ghana*, Government Printer, Accra 1967, p.30. The Commission was appointed after the July 1967 salary increase, to report on public service remuneration.
3. For an explanation of this term, see the Statistical Appendix.
4. The 'Plan', prepared by the Harvard Advisory Group, resembled more a progress report, and it was not heard of again.
5. The reorientation of the economy away from a socialist model towards a more orthodox Western system, the emphasis on private enterprise, and the general moves towards better economic management were expected to bring some tangible benefits in the form of increased foreign investment. The NLC made a number of specific moves to encourage such investment, including greater freedom for the repatriation of profits and adherence to the International Convention on the protection of investments. During the NLC's term of office, these moves had no more effect on the flow of private capital than those of Nkrumah. The most substantial investment that was made – the Kaiser aluminium smelter – had already been negotiated before 1966. The other major investments were attracted as part of the early efforts to denationalise state industries. Overall, the net flow of long-term private capital for

direct investment during 1966–69, at £45m., was roughly balanced by the outflow of dividends and profits. The Abbott affair (see Section 2) played some part in discouraging potential investors, as well as putting the NLC on guard about the terms it was prepared to offer. However, by far the biggest disincentive to the expatriate investor appeared to be the lack of identifiable opportunities, particularly in a period of general uncertainty about the long-term prospects of the economy. In 1970, the World Bank could not see any prospect of Ghana being able to attract considerable amounts of private capital from overseas for many years to come.

Chapter 7 Summary and Lessons

1. Nkrumah's economic programme

At the time of Nkrumah's downfall in early 1966, Ghana was unable to meet its foreign debt commitments. Even without the burden of debt-service payments, the economy was on a downward slide. The policies which foreign credits both sustained and encouraged had brought the government's finances and the balance of payments to the brink of collapse. These credits had been taken up entirely since 1959, and mostly in the four years before Nkrumah's downfall. But their roots – and with it the real roots of the debt problem – are to be found in a much earlier period, roughly that between the founding of the United Gold Coast Convention in 1947 and the publication of the Lewis Report in 1953.

Then the combination of the economic discontent of the masses and the political agitation of the intelligentsia focussed attention on the fragility of Ghana's economic structure, despite its high income in the African context. It also helped to associate, in the minds of many Ghanaians, economic backwardness with colonial rule. Nkrumah thus came to political power at a time of reaction against the caution of the colonial authorities, and against the colonial economy with its dependence on volatile primary export markets. This was also a time when planning and industrialisation were becoming fashionable concepts as 'ways out' of under-development. So Nkrumah's economic policy was one of planned 'restructuring' away from the colonial economy through massive public investment, with the eventual aim of reaching the status of an industrial society. The high level of Ghana's foreign reserves, swelled by the post-war boom in the cocoa market, allowed Nkrumah to make a quick start towards this goal.

The concept of economic 'restructuring', however, failed to be translated into an effective strategy until the Seven-Year Plan, by which time it was too late. In the beginning, restructuring was pursued merely by accelerating the public investment programmes inherited from the colonial Ten-Year Plan; but still greater emphasis was put on building up the infrastructure and expanding the public service, partly with the deliberate aim of creating the foundations for industrial development, and partly because it was easiest to speed up programmes in the traditional areas of government endeavour. Up to about 1954, the acceleration in public investment, by clearing the back-log of high priority improvements in the infrastructure, made an important and rapid contribution to raising economic productivity and the economy's capacity for further growth. Thereafter, however, growth in GDP was increasingly sustained by boosts to demand from public spending, which was financed more and more from accumulated reserves. By the time of independence, there were few signs that public investment had made any lasting contribution to modernising the traditional sectors – particularly food growing – or had encouraged the setting up of modern industry, either by Ghanaian or by foreign enterprise.

Attempts were made in 1957, and again through the Five-Year Plan in 1959, to reduce the lag between public investment and production in agriculture or industry by redirecting public resources to what were considered to be more directly productive schemes. But growth continued, in practice, to be sustained largely by the high level of demand created by public spending. The balance of payments crisis of 1961 – when a massive current account deficit brought Ghana's foreign exchange reserves down to a level dangerously low for a country whose export earnings were prone to extreme fluctuations – should have brought to an end the policy of relying on massive public sector spending. Instead, Ghana embarked on a still more ambitious public investment programme, hoping to correct the payments disequilibrium, raise output generally, and salvage the 'restructuring' objective by programmes of import-substitution and export diversification through state farms and state-owned industries. At the same time, however, no brake was put on other investments in infrastructure and social services[1], and these increased at an even faster rate than before.

This decision was only possible because Ghana had secured a large number of medium-term credits and Eastern loans and was confident of securing still more. During 1962–5, however, even the massive use of such credits did not allow it to finance all government spending and all its imports without recourse to short-term expedients, such as deficit financing and short-term borrowing from abroad.

Medium-term credits, while allowing the government to start more projects than its own financial resources allowed, helped to expand the public investment programme beyond the country's capacity, to execute it properly. Since the credits covered only a part of the capital costs of projects, and in balance of payments terms at best only the direct foreign exchange costs of plant and equipment, they also put an additional strain on the budget and the country's foreign exchange position. If the projects financed in this way could have contributed quickly to output, and thereby to revenue and foreign exchange earnings (or savings), these strains would have been avoided. But they did not — partly because Ghana chose the wrong projects, partly because it allowed itself to be talked into the wrong projects by suppliers eager for contracts, and partly because much of the latter's work was incompetent and much of their equipment unsuited or defective. The terms on which the credits were offered finally precipitated, but did not in themselves cause, the debt crisis which Nkrumah's successors inherited.

2. The debt

In 1966 the foreign debt, including interest, amounted to £255m. Payments due to be made by Ghana in the five years from 1966 to 1970 totalled £163m. Of this, £40m. was in short-term debt, which was postponed — indefinitely in effect — through a 'revolving' credit agreement with exporters and IMF stand-by credits. Roughly another £8m. owed to Eastern countries was subject to a moratorium negotiated by Nkrumah just before his downfall. This left a hard-core debt on medium- and long-term credits due in 1966–70 of £115m., or £23m. a year.

What sort of burden did this impose on the economy? On medium- and long-term credits alone, the debt ratio looked like falling somewhere in the range of 12.5–18 percent, assuming export earnings at the 1965 level (for the higher figure), or rising during 1966–70 to an average of 50 percent over the 1965 level (for the lower figure). In a well-run and growing economy, with rising exports, the lower ratio would have been manageable. In Ghana's case, however, both real GDP per head and export earnings had been stagnant during the previous four years. In the future, earnings from aluminium exports were expected to boost the total, but in view of Ghana's continued dependence on cocoa, which was then on a downward market, it was unlikely that anything like a 50 percent increase could be achieved. Moreover, Ghana's balance of payments on current goods and services had been in deficit by an average of £9m. in 1962–5. Even so, the level of imports had not been sufficient to avoid serious shortages of both essential consumer goods and raw materials, components, or spare parts needed in production. Some reduction in public spending — which would have benefitted the economy in any case – would have eased the demand for imports; but because consumer imports had been severely curtailed through controls, this reduction could not be relied on to bring down the import bill substantially. Ghana's room for manoeuvre was, in effect, severely limited by two of the more long-term legacies of the Nkrumah era – the lag in the growth rate of marketed crops behind that of the urban population, and the increasing dependence of output on imports through the development of import-intensive manufactures. The former made food imports progressively more difficult to contain; the latter made rising maintenance imports a prerequisite of growth in an increasing number of establishments. Consequently, the diversion of £23m. of foreign exchange a year from imports to debt-service payments would inevitably have turned stagnation into deep recession.

As a result of a series of international and bilateral negotiations with its creditors, Ghana's debt-service payments in 1966–70 were effectively reduced from the scheduled annual average of £23m. to £11m. In addition, it received new aid of £5.5m. a year. On top of that, Ghana's total outstanding short-term debt (including IMF obligations) was allowed to rise by about £8m. a year. Nevertheless, Ghana did not avoid a major recession in 1966–8 – in these three years incomes per head continued to fall, bringing down average real GDP per head in 1968 back to its early 1960 level of £68.

The NLC had made a pledge, early in 1966, to honour the debts incurred by Nkrumah. This decision was prompted in part by moral principle; but the regime did hope, too, that it would make easier a satisfactory debt settlement and prompt a sympathetic reaction to appeals for long-term aid from Western governments. The NLC was disappointed at the debt-relief and aid arrangements it was offered – particularly in regard to the rates of interest charged on deferred debts arising from Western supplier credits; but it accepted the settlements in good grace and maintained its determination to honour all obligations to the end. The Busia administration took a more aggressive line, partly because it feared the consequences of a new recession after 1969, and partly because it faced an increase in payments on the rescheduled debts within its expected term of office. It openly questioned its ability to honour the debts at the rescheduled rate and, more important, challenged the view that the creditors, or the governments which had guaranteed the credits, could fairly deny all responsibility for the mess in which Ghana found itself.

The result of the various post-Nkrumah negotiations on aid and debt rescheduling, up to and including the interim settlement in 1970, are

Table 7.1 Summary outcome of post-Nkrumah aid and debt negotiations 1966–1970.

(£m.)[1]

	1966	1967	1968	1969	1970	Total (1966–70)	1971	1972	1973
1. Debt schedules as of Feb. 1966.									
i) Total medium & long-term	19	31	33	23	18	123.0	15	(13)	(10)
ii) Western suppliers' credits only	13.7	20.2	22.3	17.9	14.4	88.2	10.9	(7)	(5)
2. Debt schedules as of July 1970	(Actual Payments / Disbursements)						(Estimate)	(Projections)[2]	
i) Total medium & long-term	(6.0)	(5.0)	15.0	10.3	(18.2)	(54.5)	(18)	(24)	(26)
ii) Western suppliers' credits only	(4.0)	3.0	12.5	6.0	(8.1)	(33.6)	9.5	14.3	14.7
3. New aid[3]	4.0	7.2	17.1	18.8	(24.0)	(71.1)	(27)	(27)	(27)
4: Disbursements of credits in 'pipeline'[4] as of 1 January 1966	29.3	12.9	–	–	–	42.2	–	–	–
5. Net new resources (= 3 minus 2)	-2.0	2.2	2.1	8.5	5.8	16.6	(9)	(3)	(1)
6. Net short-term/IMF (change in obligations)[5]		(-30.0)	-3.0	-3.5	(-3.5)	(-40.0)	(-32)	..	..

Notes:
1. At constant £ / $ / N₵ exchange rates (i.e. as of Feb. 1966)
2. World Bank projections made in 1970.
3. Includes IMF medium-term compensatory finance loan of £6.3m, made in December 1966.
4. Largely supplier credits and Eastern loans.
5. – signifies increase in outstanding obligations (i.e. net short-term credits received by Ghana); IMF refers to stand-by credits only, see note 3.

( ) estimate on partial information.

Sources Information supplied by Ministry of Economic Affairs (External Aid Division) Accra, US AID (Accra), the World Bank and the Overseas Development Administration, London.

summarised in Table 7.1. The figures in the totals column in the middle of the table – comparing row 1(i) with row 2(i) and row 1(ii) with 2(ii) – give an instant picture of the debt relief afforded to Ghana during 1966–70 on all medium- and long-term credits, and on Western suppliers' credits, respectively. The total for row 5 shows that the net new inflow of resources (aid from all quarters minus debt service) for 1966–70 came to £16.6m. For Western countries, who were the major creditors, and now the only bilateral source of aid, the net new flow of resource was £22m. But their gross contribution (i.e. new aid of £50m. plus debt-relief on supplier credits of £55m.) totalled as much as £105m. Whether one considers that Ghana was well or badly treated in the post-Nkrumah period depends to some extent on which figure, that for the gross or net contribution, should be taken as the more appropriate measure. From Ghana's point of view the lower figure is relevant, since it represents the real contribution made to its economic recovery programme in the period in question; it represents also the net amount that Ghana would have forfeited in contributions from these countries had it reneged on its debt payments after the 1966 coup. Ghana's creditors have taken the higher figure as the effective measure of their contribution, since it represents the net amount they have foregone during 1966–70, or which they could have provided to other developing countries; but the higher figure is based on the unrealistic assumption that, Ghana would in any event have continued to meet the full debt payments as they became due. Another important factor in the equation is that the debt relief provided nevertheless had to be paid off in the near future, with an additional interest charge of £33m. on the deferred part. Payments started to rise again in 1970, and were due to rise sharply from 1972; at the same time, creditors became increasingly reluctant on further relief, and rejected Ghana's request to be given the same generous terms as they had agreed in 1970 with Indonesia in respect of its debts. While Ghana could not claim that the actual payments it was asked to make during 1966–70 were an important hindrance to economic recovery, it could argue that the series of short-term debt postponements had produced a state of perpetual uncertainty which hampered the preparation and implementation of long-term measures. The creditors believed, on the other hand, that the control, implied in the short-term nature of the settlements, provided a desirable check on Ghana's stabilisation and rehabilitation efforts. Ghana did not, certainly, show the degree of progress which might have been expected, and its government has to accept at least some of the responsibility for this. But, in the end, the attitude of the creditors, especially after 1969, and the series of prolonged debt negotiations became the scapegoats for Ghana's own shortcomings.

While no one can say with certainty what would have happened had Ghana reneged on its debts in 1966, there may be a moral for other countries in the creditors' reaction to Colonel Acheampong's declaration in January 1972 that Ghana was repudiating a part of the debt and unilaterally rescheduling the rest. Western governments have since then offered Ghana by far the most generous settlement package it has yet received.

The aspect of Western creditors' treatment of Ghana that is of widest interest to both debtors and creditors is their failure to accept any responsibility for the effect of their guarantees on the growth in Ghana's debt. Clerly the creditors' view is right – as far as it goes – that Ghana has to shoulder the main responsibility for accepting credits beyond its servicing capacity, as well as for their misuse or application to worthless projects, and the failure to supervise suppliers to ensure value for money. Nevertheless, the government agencies – such as ECGD in Britain – had willingly accepted a risk in issuing credit guarantees, guided supposedly by a commercial assessment of Ghana's credit-worthiness. This assessment turned out to be wrong. It is not unreasonable to suggest, therefore, as Mensah and others did, that these governments should have accepted at least some of the consequences of their mistakes. Embarrassment would have been avoided – and Ghana well served – if they had originally succeeded in reading correctly Ghana's economic situation in 1962–5.

How the guaranteeing agencies managed to misread Ghana's situation remains a puzzle. In response to Ghana's deteriorating balance of payments position in 1961, several of them – including Britain's Export Credit Guarantee Department – restricted their cover on medium-term credits. This did not, however, prevent a massive build-up of guaranteed credit contracts into 1965. Only then was effective action taken – when it was too late – and ECGD, for one, still shunned the extreme measure of suspending cover altogether. While guarantees continued to be issued in greater numbers during 1963 and 1964, the World Bank and the IMF were refusing further help to Ghana. The IMF repeated its warning annually, starting in 1962, that Ghana should first curtail, and then avoid, the use of medium-term finance. Moreover, Nkrumah was widely held up at the time as an example of an incompetent and irresponsible leader pushing the country into chaos. And in 1964 even the Russians, despite their political commitment, were becoming disenchanted.

The only mitigating factor is the time-lag between the initiation of project discussions and the point at which actual guarantees are sought. Normally one credit contract required the co-operation and agreement of more than two parties. On many projects several foreign companies were involved, each responsible for only one part of the project (civil engineering work, supply of equipment, etc.). Agreement in principle first had to be reached between the Ghana government and the various companies involved, each of which then had to secure credit from one or more sources. Therefore, by the time the guaranteeing agencies came into the picture, a great deal of time had been spent in negotiating and assembling a total package. The guaranteeing agencies were reluctant to veto deals at the eleventh hour. In any event none of them was really in a position to have accurate advance warning of the volume of contracts in the pipeline which could come up for guarantee, either in their own country or even less so in other countries. In Britain's case the surge of new credit contracts coming up for guarantee in 1963 and 1964 was, certainly to some extent, a consequence of the wave of negotiations which had been initiated in rather better times for Ghana. It is also likely that the reduced flow in 1965 was a consequence of reduced interest in initiating *new* credit deals with Ghana during 1963 and 1964, which itself may have been affected by the 1961 restrictions imposed by ECGD.

Since the debt repudiation of 1972 all cover has been suspended, and before that, in 1966, Ghana and its creditors had agreed that no further medium-term supplier finance should be accepted.[2] For Ghana, the guarantee issue is for the time being a problem of the past. But other developing countries, many of them with rising debt ratios, continue to accept such credits, and these often carry creditor government guarantees. One of the reasons behind the creditors' reluctance to bail Ghana out, not only quickly but also 'permanently', has been the wish to demonstrate to others that there is no easy way out of debt, and that relief carries certain penalties. They may have succeeded. But there remains the need to find effective ways of discouraging countries from getting into a bad debt situation in the first place. One way would be for creditor governments to exercise greater selectivity and toughness in the matter of credit cover. However, this approach requires full co-operation between creditor governments and their respective insuring agencies, and some common rules of procedure. Otherwise, restraint on the part of one country would merely put its exporters at a disadvantage without necessarily influencing the total volume of available credit. It requires also a more adequate warning system on the build-up of debt and of supplier finance in individual developing countries. A tentative step towards a common approach to medium-term supplier credit (and its official insurance), and towards finding out if workable (common) guidelines can be drawn up for credit rating, was taken at the Development Assistance Committee (OECD) High-Level meeting in the autumn of 1972. This is a small but important step, which, if it can lead to some measure of agreement, would help both creditor and debtor countries: the former by minimising the risk of bad debts; the latter by reducing the damage inflicted on their countries by bad credit management. And it would also help other developing countries – those showing self-restraint and prudence – by reducing the chances of aid funds (actual or potential) being absorbed in rescue operations for countries failing to show similar restraint.

Notes

1. The Volta Project, to which the World Bank, the United States and Britain contributed just under half the cost, was the most spectacular of these.
2. Ghana did, however, accept one supplier credit valued at £0.4m. in 1971.

Statistical Appendix

1. Note on Ghana's statistics

The Watson Report of 1948 noted Ghana's 'almost complete lack of statistics'. This criticism, and the subsequent needs of government in preparing the Ten-Year Plan, provided new stimuli to the systematic collection and presentation of official statistics. Major steps forward included the pioneering work on the National Income by Seers and Ross in 1952 and the subsequent calculations for 1950–55 (made with the assistance of a UN expert) and published in the Economic Survey for 1955. Since then the statistical coverage has improved steadily, with 1960–62 being particularly important because of the completion of the Population Census, the Walters National Income Survey (see notes on Sources) and linked Household Expenditure Survey, the Industrial Census and the Preliminary Agricultural Census.

Despite the improvements, major gaps remain, and the reliability and accuracy of many of the series is still suspect; on both counts there has been, moreover, a decline since the mid-1960s, and particularly since 1969. Ghanaian statistics should not be considered, therefore, as more than indicators of relative magnitudes and of trends.

The statistics presented in this study are derived mainly from published official sources. In some cases these have been supplemented by either published private research findings, or unpublished material (official and private) made available during interviews.

One academic work which proved particularly valuable as a guide to statistical sources is *A Study of Contemporary Ghana,* edited by W. Birmingham, I. Neustadt and E.N. Omaboe (Allen and Unwin, 1966). Among official Ghana publications, most extensive use has been made of the following: (1) the plan documents (Ten-Year, Five-Year, Seven-Year and Two-Year Plans); (2) the regular repots of Government Departments and Public Corporations, particularly the Economic Surveys (published by the Ministry of Finance, and after 1958 by the Central Statistical Office); and (3) occasional reports of judicial enquiries or foreign advisory missions (referred to in the text).

Ghanaian statistics refer either to calendar years, or to (cocoa) crop-years (Oct.–Sept.) or financial years. The dates of the latter have been changed frequently; up to 1954–5 the financial year ran from April to March; in 1955–6 it was extended by three months, to run subsequently from July to June; in 1961–2 it was again extended, to run subsequently from October to September; in 1965 it was changed to a calendar year basis and in mid-1966 back to a July–June basis. Between 1950 and 1969 there have therefore been three financial 'years' of fifteen months duration, and one of six months; and the dates have changed seven times. So as to make figures more immediately comparable over time, all financial and crop-year data have been converted here to a calendar year basis. In the conversion some distortion of figures as between one year and the next has been unavoidable; these are not big, and in the summary tables in the Appendix, where average figures each covering four years are used, they are insignificant.

2. Currency and exchange rates

During the period covered there were a number of changes in the currency unit used in Ghana. Up to July 1965 the basic unit of account was the Ghana Pound, freely convertible into, and equivalent in value to, the Pound Sterling. The Ghana Pound was then succeeded by the Cedi (£1 = ₵2.4), divided into 100 Pesewas (each equivalent to one penny in the old currency). After the 1966 coup, the NLC introduced the New Cedi (£1 = N₵2). In July 1967 the New Cedi was devalued by 30 percent against Sterling (to £1 = N₵2.85). In December 1971 the Cedi was again devalued by 48.6 percent, and in January 1972 revalued by 42 percent. The rate in effect at the end of 1972 was N₵1 = $0.78 = £0.32.

In the study all money values are expressed in a fixed unit equivalent in value to the old Ghana Pound i.e. £1 = £G1 = N₵2 (or, after the Cedi devaluation in 1967, £1 = N₵2.85 before the 1967 *Sterling* devaluation, and £1 = N₵2.45 after the Sterling devaluation). A fixed exchange rate unit is used for convenience in a period of changing parities; also the exchange rate (£1 = N₵2) is that which applied throughout the Nkrumah period during which the debt was incurred, and in many of the sources cited – including the three plan documents – values are expressed in Ghana Pounds. All figures relating to the period after the devaluation of the New Cedi have been converted to their pre-devaluation equivalents so as to make comparisons with the Nkrumah period easier. To obtain pre-devaluation equivalents, items originally denominated in New Cedis (e.g. domestic output) have been divided by the old Cedi/Sterling exchange rate (i.e. by 2); items whose New Cedi value merely reflects conversion at the new exchange rate from figures originally denominated in other currencies (e.g. exports and external debt) have been divided by the post-1967 devaluation exchange rate (i.e. by 2.85).

Care must be taken, when comparing *the figures shown in this study* with those obtained from other sources, to check that the relevant exchange rate is used. For equivalence with other source figures published betwen July 1967 and December 1972 (the months of the two Cedi devaluations) and expressed in Dollars, Cedis or Pounds Sterling, the following conversion rates should be used, rather than the current exchange rates:

Figures expressed in	*Date figures compiled*	*Conversion factor*
$	July 1967 – Dec.1972	0.36
N₵	July 1967 – Oct.1967	0.35
	Nov.1967 – Dec.1971	0.40
	(Feb.1972 – Dec.1972)	(0.32)
£ (UK sources relating to UK transactions)	All dates	1.00
£ (IMF/IBRD sources relating to all transactions and already converted from $)	Up to Oct.1967	1.00
	Nov.1967 – Dec.1972	

It should be noted that figures expressed in all the above currencies contain a slight upward bias since 1966 due to the net appreciation of the German Mark, Dutch Guilder and French Franc (as a group) relative to the other currencies. Finally, it should be noted that figures expressed in Pounds, Dollars and Credis, and compiled since August 1971, are affected by the general currency realignment which has occurred since then.

3. Source for Appendix and other Tables

Appendix Tables

Table A1 – Population and labour force: Censuses of 1948, 1960, 1970; inter-census years by straight-line interpolation. Paid employment (recorded): up to 1960 *Annual Labour Statistics*; after 1960, *Economic Surveys* (Employment); (unrecorded): 1958–61, census; 1966–69, World Bank estimate; other years estimated from partial coverage in *Labour Statistics*. Earnings: calculated from figures given in 'An Index of the Real Wages of the Unskilled Labourer in Accra', W. Birmingham, *Economic Bulletin of Ghana*, March 1960; Mills – Odoi Report, op. cit., pp.31–33; *Economic Surveys* (Sections on Wages and Earnings; Prices).

Table A2 – Up to 1954: *Ghana: Projected Level of Demand, Supply and Imports of Agricultural Products in 1965, 1970 and 1975,* by H. Ord *et al.*, Dept. of Agriculture, Washington, 1965; figures calculated on the same basis as used in the Walters Report (see below). After 1954: *Report on the National Accounts of Ghana 1955–61*, by D. Walters, Government Printer, Accra, 1962; and series continued in *Economic Surveys* (Economic Conditions in Ghana and Annex).

Table A3 – The figures have been estimated from a variety of sources (see below), using the methodology set out in the Walters Report (Annex on Sources and Methodology). They are not to be taken as more than a *very rough* guide to the changing pattern of sectoral incomes. For 1950–54, D. Seers and C. Ross *Financial and Physical Problems of Development in the Gold Coast*, Government Printer, Accra, (figures covering 1949–51) supplemented by estimates of cocoa, agricultural and mining incomes derived from figures given in *Economic Surveys,* the Five and Seven-Year Plans and Birmingham, *et al.*, op. cit., Chs.9–11 for 1955–61: Walters Report; for 1962–64, estimated from production figures for cocoa, agriculture, mining, industry and construction given in *Economic Surveys*, the Industrial Census and the Preliminary Agricultural Census; for 1965–69, *Economic Survey for Africa*, ECA, French Edition, 1970, supplemented by estimates from production figures for cocoa, agriculture, mining, industry and construction in *Economic Surveys*, and from World Bank estimates.

Tables A5, A6 and A8 – Budget revenue and expenditure (corrected and revised figures) *Economic Surveys*, 1966 and 1969, Statistical Annex. Recurrent and capital expenditure; up to 1953, derived from Budget Estimates, 1954–61, from *Seven-Year Development Plan*, Table 13.3; after 1961, *Economic Surveys*, Statistical Annex. Total expenditure under Central Government Control: as above; plus Annual Reports of Public Corporations; Ministry of Economic Affairs unpublished figures on aid, Eastern loans and suppliers' credits.

Table A7 – *Economic Surveys* (Sections on Central Government and Supplementary Tables/Statistical Annex).

Table A9 – Exports and Imports at constant and current prices: up to 1954, H. Ord *et al.* op. cit.; after 1954, *Economic Surveys* (Statistical Annex). Composition of exports and end-use of imports: *Economic Surveys.*

Table A10 – Capital movements and reserves: up to 1960, Birmingham *et al.*, op. cit., Tables 14.11, 14.12; after 1960, *Economic Surveys* (Section on Balance of Payments and Statistical Annex).

Tables in the text (supplementary note on sources)

Tables 3.1, 4.2 and 4.3 (see also below) – as for Table A5.

Tables 4.3 and 4.4 (see also above) – The two main sources for information on supplier credits and Eastern loans are: (1) The Budget 1966–67, Financial Statement (Annex Table IX), Government Printer, Accra; and (2) *Developments in the Ghanaian Economy between 1960 and 1968*, Ministry of Economic Affairs, Accra, 1969. These were supplemented by information received from the Ministry of Economic Affairs. The main sources for aid are (2) above and information received from the World Bank, USAID (Accra) and Overseas Development Administration, London.

Table A 1. Trends in employment 1950 – 1969

(annual averages, 000's)

	1950–53	1954–57	1958–61	1962–65	1966–69
Approximate Population	5,300	5,900	6,600	7,400	8,200
Labour force [1]	2,150	(2,400)	2,700	(3,000)	3,300
Wage & salary earners:					
Public sector	98	132	144	252	278
Private Sector (recorded) [2]	107	123	136	122	104
Private Sector (unrecorded) [3]	(120)	(145)	185	(136)	96
Total	(325)	(400)	465	(510)	478
Share in labour force (%)	(15)	(16)	17	(17)	15
Farmers, self-employed employers and family workers	(1,825)	(2,200)	2,335	(2,485)	2,822
Average earnings from paid employment (£ monthly)	..	11.10	14.08	17.03	23.00
Index of real earnings (1955 = 100)	..	113	137	122	145
Minimum wage (£ monthly) [4]	6.20	6.75	8.10	8.10	9.45
Index of real wages (1952 = 100)	95	107	119	99	..

Notes:

1. Population over 15, excluding 'homemakers', students, old people and voluntarily unemployed.
2. Largely urban employees in establishments with more than 10 paid employees; 'agricultural' employment is largely confined to forestry and fishing.
3. Small establishments and full-time paid workers in cocoa farming.
4. Going rate up to July 1960; legal minimum thereafter.

Sources: The table and other statistics in this chapter are based on a wide variety of sources of different degrees of reliability. These are listed in the statistical note in the Appendix, with some additional comments on the figures.

Table A 2. Gross Domestic Product, 1950–1969

(annual averages)

	1950–53	1954–57	1958–61	1962–65	1966–69
At current market prices					
GDP (£m.)	260	340	450	660	990
At constant (1960) prices					
GDP (£m.)	289	356	446	540	572
Growth rate (%)	3.0	6.4	6.4	3.1	1.6
GDP per caput (£)	55	61	68	73	69
Growth rate (%)	0.2	3.6	3.4	0.1	-1.4
Components of GDP at constant prices [1]					
Domestic Expenditure (£m.)	269	362	468[1]	537	556[1]
Consumption (£m.)	231	305	381	429	471
Share in Domestic Exp (%)	85.9	84.3	81.4	79.9	84.8
Per caput (£)	44	52	58	58	57
Growth rate (%)	0.6	4.4	3.7	-3.3	-0.4
Investment (£m.)	38	57	84	108	81
Share in Domestic Exp. (%)	14.1	15.7	18.0	20.1	14.7
Share in GDP (%)	13.1	16.0	18.9	20.0	14.2
Savings (£m.)	58	51	65	111	100
Share in GDP (%)	20.0	14.4	14.6	20.5	17.4
External balance (£m.)[2]	20	-6	-22	3	16

Notes: 1. Domestic Expenditure = Domestic Investment plus change in stocks plus consumption. The discrepancy in 1958–61 and 1962–65 is explained by changes in stocks.
GDP = Domestic Expenditure plus external net balance.

2. External balance = Exports minus imports (of goods and services, but excluding transfer payments).

Sources: See note to Table A 1.

Table A 3. Sectoral structure of incomes 1950–1969 (percentage shares in GDP at factor cost) [1]

	1950–53	1954–57	1958–61	1962–65	1966–69
Agriculture [2]	35.0	36.0	34.0	31.5	33.0
Cocoa	19.0	17.0	15.0	14.0	13.0
Mining	5.5	5.0	4.5	3.5	3.5
Industry	4.0	5.0	7.5	11.5	14.0
Construction	6.5	6.5	7.0	7.0	4.5
Services [3]	30.0	30.5	32.0	33.0	32.0
Total GDP (£m.)	280	340	420	500	530

Notes:

1. GDP at factor cost = GDP at market prices minus indirect taxes plus subsidies. The income shares given here are calculated on the basis of money incomes deflated by a price (cost of living) index. They do not reflect the relative value of output at constant prices. The changing export price for cocoa is therefore taken into account in this table.

2. Includes forestry, fishing and animal husbandry. Incomes earned in food crop cultivation include value of local processing and distribution, which are thought to account for 30 percent of the total.

3. Includes all incomes other than those from listed sectors, i.e. largely government service, commerce and trade, transport, personal services.

Sources: See note to Table A 1.

Table A 4. The public sector in the economy 1950–1969[1] (annual averages, constant 1960 prices)

	1950–53	1954–57	1958–61	1962–65	1966–69
Public consumption (£m.)	20.5	34.7	45.5	67.2	100.2
share in total consumption (%)	8.9	11.4	11.9	15.6	21.3
share in GDP (%)	7.0	9.7	10.2	12.4	17.6
Public investment (£m.)	13.7	21.1	35.3	77.8	(42.0)
share in total investment (%)	36.0	37.0	42.0	72.0	(52.0)
share in GDP (%)	4.7	6.0	8.0	14.4	(7.4)
Public Sector total (£m.)	34.2	55.8	80.8	145.0	(142.2)
share in GDP (%)	11.7	15.7	18.2	26.8	(25.0)

Notes: 1. **Goods and services according to National Accounts classification (thus excluding transfer payments). Includes such expenditure by all government agencies and Public Corporations. For 1966–69 the division between public and private investment is only approximate; the figure for the total size of the public sector is therefore also only approximate.**

Sources: See note to Table A 1.

Table A 5. Changes in the sectoral distribution of public expenditure 1950–1969[1]
(percentages in total)

	1950–53	1954–57	1958–61	1962–65	1966–69
Agriculture[2]	11.8	11.4	8.8	9.4	9.1
recurrent	14.7	13.4	11.1	8.8	8.5
capital	5.2	5.8	5.5	10.0	11.5
Manufacturing & Mining	2.0	2.5	8.6	13.8	5.0
recurrent	1.4	1.3	2.0	3.0	2.9
capital	2.9	5.0	18.5	24.2	13.5
Infrastructure & Public Services [3]	26.5	25.8	24.6	26.6	13.7
recurrent	16.4	16.8	14.0	12.5	6.9
capital	44.0	45.8	40.5	40.1	37.7
Education	16.3	14.4	11.5	15.7	22.6
recurrent	16.7	15.6	13.8	26.2	26.3
capital	16.1	11.7	8.0	5.5	9.3
Health, Housing & Social Services [4]	15.3	14.2	12.6	11.9	16.1
recurrent	17.5	14.3	13.4	16.4	17.3
capital	11.6	13.8	11.3	7.5	11.8
General Government Administration [5]	27.6	31.8	32.2	22.0	32.9
recurrent	33.3	38.6	45.7	33.1	38.1
capital	20.2	17.9	16.4	12.7	16.2
Actual expenditure (£m.)	31	53	96	172	(176)-
recurrent (£m.)	19	33	58	85	116
capital (£m.)	12	19	38	87	(60)

Notes:

1. This table is based on public expenditure directly controlled by Central Government (see Table 6). It excludes interest on foreign debt, the expenditure of Public Corporations and Local Authorities out of their own incomes (and to a small extent, domestic borrowing). The table covers more than 90 percent of total public sector investment, corresponding roughly to that part which is included in the investment allocations under successive development plans. The figures for 1966–69 are based on less complete coverage; they probably underestimate 'infrastructure' and 'manufacturing'.
2. Expenditure made by the CMB is not included.
3. Public Services include electricity and water.
4. Includes public housing, sanitation; Social Services includes social benefits in cash.
5. This comprises the general cost of Central Government (including Civil Service salaries); also police, law and prisons, etc. and grants to Local Authorities for general services.

Sources: See note to Table A 1.

Table A 6. Sectoral distribution of public investment under the Ten-Year, Five-Year and Seven-Year Plans and in the post-Nkrumah Period.
(percentage shares in total)

	Ten-Year [1] Plan (1951–1958)	Five-Year [2] Plan (1959–1963)	Seven-Year [3] Plan (1964–1965)	Post [4] Nkrumah (1966–1969)
Agriculture	6	7	10	12
Manufacturing & Mining	4	21	26	13
Infrastructure & Public Services	45	32	41	38
Education	13	9	5	9
Health, Social & Housing	13	13	7	12
General Government	19	18	12	16
Total	100	100	100	100
Total Investment (£m.) (annual averages)	15.5	51.6	108.0	(60.0) [5]

Notes:
1. Covers period from starting date of the Ten-Year Plan to the end of 1958, thus including 18 months of the Consolidation period.
2. Period originally intended to be covered by the Five-Year Plan.
3. First two years of Seven-Year Plan.
4. Includes two months covered by the Seven-Year Plan (Jan.–Feb. 1966).
5. Estimate.

Sources: See note to Table A 1.

Table A 7. Composition of government revenue 1950–1969. (annual averages)

	1950–53	1954–57	1958–61	1962–65	1966–69
Total revenue (£m.)	33.6	53.7	73.6	106.5	139.2
Revenue to GDP (%)	13	17	15	18	21
Taxes to GDP (%) [1]	13	16	14	15	19
Composition of revenue (Percentages in total)					
Cocoa duty	41	45	27	12	19
CMB contributions [2]	4	5	9	4	–
Total from cocoa	45	50	36	16	19
Taxes on:					
Income & wealth	16	10	10	17	20
Imports	27	27	28	36	23
Goods & services [3]	2	3	7	15	25
Miscellaneous revenue [1] (excluding CMB)	10	10	19	16	13

Notes:

1. The difference between total revenue and taxes is miscellaneous revenue, which includes fees for services, rents, fines, etc. (and CMB contributions).
2. Cocoa Marketing Board grants, special development contributions and compulsory savings paid on behalf of cocoa farmers and deducted from payments due on cocoa deliveries to the CMB by farmers.
3. Excise duties and purchase taxes.

Sources: See note to Table A 1.

Table A 8. Summary of Central Government budgetary position 1950–1969.
(annual averages, current prices £m.)

	1950–53	1954–57	1958–61	1962–65	1966–69
Expenditure under direct control of Central Government (excluding interest)	31.0	52.0	96.0	172.0	(176.0)
Financed outside Budget[1]	2.7	2.8	9.4	25.8	(23.5)
Carried in the Budget	28.3	49.2	86.6	146.2	152.5
Interest on debt	0.4	0.7	1.1	4.5	12.5
Total Budget expenditure[2]	28.7	49.9	87.7	150.7	165.0
Total Revenue[2]	33.6	53.5	73.6	106.5	139.2
Budget surplus/deficit	4.6	3.6	-14.1	-44.1	-25.8
Current expenditure	19.0	33.9	58.9	89.8	129.0
Capital expenditure	9.7	16.0	28.8	60.9	36.0
Central Government saving[3]	14.4	19.6	14.7	16.7	10.2
as proportion of capital expenditure (%)	148	122	51	27	30

Notes:

1. Borrowing on behalf of Public Corporations: includes also supplier credits for projects not included in Central Government Estimates and aid for the Volta River Project.
2. Revenue and budget expenditure exclude Central Government loans (and loan repayments received).
3. Saving taken to mean revenue minus recurrent expenditure.

Sources: See note to Table A 1.

Table A 9. Ghana's foreign trade 1950–1969 (annual averages)

	1950–53		1954–57		1958–61		1962–65		1966–69	
	(£m.)	Share in GDP (%)	(£m.)	Share in GDP (%)	(£m.)	Share in GDP (%)	(£m.)	Share in GDP (%)	(£m.)	Share in GDP (%)
Exports (goods & services)										
At constant 1960 prices	86	30	92	26	116	26	155	29	119	21
At current prices	85	33	101	30	119	26	122	18	127	13
Imports (goods & services)										
At constant 1960 prices	66	23	99	28	138	31	152	28	105	18
At current prices	68	27	94	28	133	29	152	23	134	14
Composition of exports of goods	(£m.)	Share in total (%)	(£m.)	Share in total (%)	(£m.)	Share in total (%)	(£m.)	Share in total (%)	(£m.)	Share in total (%)
Cocoa	56.1	66	63.3	62	67.3	57	72.3	60	74.3	58
Minerals	20.8	24	23.1	23	26.8	22	21.7	18	21.3	17
Timber	5.0	6	8.9	9	13.8	11	13.1	11	11.5	9
Total above	81.9	96	95.3	94	107.9	90	107.1	89	107.1	84
Other exports	3.1	4	5.7	6	11.1	10	14.9	11	19.9	16
Imports by end use										
Food	11.2	17	13.9	16	16.5	14	13.9	11	13.1	11
Other consumer goods	24.7	39	34.2	40	42.8	37	36.8	28	23.4	20
Building materials	20.7	32	10.0	12	13.4	12	19.6	15	13.9	12
Other intermediate goods			15.9	18	22.4	19	28.1	21	38.2	32
Capital goods	7.6	12	12.0	14	22.1	19	33.5	25	30.3	24
Total imports of goods	64.2	100	86.0	100	117.2	100	131.9	100	118.9	100
Services from abroad	3.8	–	8.0	–	15.8	–	20.1	–	15.1	–

Sources: See note to Table A 1.

Table A 10. Summary of the balance of payments and reserve positions 1950–1969
(annual averages, current prices, £m.)

	1950–53	1954–57	1958–61	1962–65	1966–69
Net exports of goods & services	17.2	7.2	−14.2	−30.7	−7.2
Net factor income & transfers	−3.2	−3.5	−7.5	−15.8	−9.6
Current balance [1]	14.0	3.7	−21.7	−46.5	−16.8
Long-term capital (net) [2]	−1.2	2.8	−0.2[2]	33.8	21.9
Short term capital & unrecorded transactions [3]	6.4	−3.7	−0.5	−6.3	1.4
Change in external reserves [4]	−19.2	−2.8	+22.4	+19.0	(−6.5)[5]
Average value of reserve holdings	140	192	142	37	−24
equivalent to import bill (months)	24.5	25.0	14.0	3.0	–

Notes:

1. This is the current price equivalent of the external balance in 1960 prices, shown in Table 2.
2. Includes private and official. The figure for 1958–61 includes £14m. capital payments on official account made in 1960 (compensation for nationalised gold mines) and 1961 (aid to Mali and Guinea).
3. Excludes 180-day trade credits and some bilateral trade credits.
4. A minus sign indicates additions to external reserve, a plus sign disinvestment.
5. Shows net use of IMF credits.

Sources: See note to Table A 1.

Index

www.ingramcontent.com/pod-product-compliance
Lightning Source LLC
LaVergne TN
LVHW021107300926
849160LV00009B/648

* 9 7 8 0 4 1 5 8 4 8 3 5 0 *